WEALTH, RICHES & MONEY

BIBLICAL PRINCIPLES OF FINANCE

BY
CRAIG HILL
&
EARL PITTS

Family Foundations Publishing
P.O. Box 320
Littleton, Colorado 80160

Cover design by
Counterpoint Design (www.counterpointdesign.com)

Printed in the United States of America

Scripture quotations are taken from: *The New King James Bible*, Thomas Nelson Publishers, 1982; *The Amplified Bible*, Zondervan Bible Publishers, 1965, 12th Printing, 1975.

The characters in many of the examples cited in this book are real life people whom the authors have known. For their privacy, however, their names and some of the insignificant details have been altered. Alternatively, some incidents described are not sequential events, but are composites of several incidents; nevertheless, they reflect very real situations.

FOREWORD

Thank God for this book. I found its message extremely helpful in my own life. I have served as a missionary for thirty years now and have been a steward of several enterprises. During this time I have learned... and forgotten many lessons. It is therefore imperative that I recover a thorough understanding of this subject in order to coach my children as they come of age and take responsibility for their own finances. Thank you Craig and Earl for summarizing the whole counsel of God on the subject in one powerful teaching.

Wealth, Riches & Money is no quick look at the basic principles of finance. Rather it is a deeply insightful journey through the scripture, including an analysis of the spiritual dynamics taking place in the unseen realm. There is an exposure of the spirit of Mammon, a demonic overlay that seeks to manipulate human attitudes toward money.

We know that money is simply a receptacle for deferred goods and services created by human cultures for trading. The mode of exchange is what we receive for our products and our time, being neither good nor evil. However the authors point out that an idolatrous reverence for the power of money becomes an enslaving deception.

The pursuit of money has become the organizing principle for society and the determining factor in personal and family decision-making. This system of thoughts and habits is so pervasive that it is impossible to live above its persuasive power without the renewing of our minds and the enabling of the Holy Spirit. We need all the help we can get from mentors who will open the scriptures to us and teach us how to live.

Craig and Earl explore the stark contrast between the Kingdom of God and the kingdom of darkness as it relates to finance, pointing out that the basic operating principle in God's economy is giving and receiving rather than buying and selling.

This principle and related truths will revolutionize your life as you understand and apply what the Bible really teaches.

Full of practical wisdom that flows from profound understanding of the character of God, the text constantly builds faith even as it imparts knowledge. These two men are true friends of God, mature Christian leaders who keep reminding us that basic provision for our lives is made by our heavenly Father, just because He loves us. Great stories, clear Bible teaching and honest personal testimony make this book accessible to everybody. I'll use it as a means to teach my children, but it would serve just as well the needs of a financial seminar for executives or the leadership team of a church.

John Dawson
Founder, International Reconciliation Coalition
Los Angeles, 2001

ENDORSEMENTS

Within the scheme of God's creation, the church is intended to be a divine agent; we are called and designed to manifest His glory in the earth. Although we are called to make the gospel of the Kingdom relevant to every aspect of life, we operate to the contrary. The circles of morality, family, personal spirituality, and social interaction are familiar to the people of God, and we operate comfortably in those circles, according to the mores of the day. Though we conform to social mores, we have failed miserably as Kingdom representatives.

The workplace, civil affairs, business and finance are looked upon as arenas where the Body of Christ should keep quiet; we conform to the mores without looking for God's Kingdom perspective.

Our great commission, though clearly relayed by Jesus, has become muddled because we are not aggressively involved as catalysts to funnel the world's resources into His Kingdom system. However, we expect to win the world without speaking the language or understanding the unchanging principles that govern their system.

Churches are swimming in debt and paying exorbitant interest that inevitably finances the kingdoms of this world. We have congregations, drowning in debt and struggling on a month-to-month basis as they try to determine how and if they are going to support the local church. Ultimately, we birth generation after generation of slaves who will be consistently oppressed by the world's economic system.

There is a clarion voice in the midst of this mayhem declaring that we can be educated to change the world of finance. These men believe we can deal faithfully, learn to manage finances and grow to a Kingdom understanding of money.

Earl Pitts and Craig Hill, through their book *Wealth, Riches & Money*, enlightens the reader by discussing basic truths that relate to the world of finance, the principles of finance, God's divine purpose for finances and how worldly finances can be converted for use in His Kingdom. *Wealth, Riches & Money* is a must read for those who are determined to see His Kingdom Come and His Will be done on earth as it is in heaven!

Amazed by His Grace,

Bishop Eddie L. Long
Senior Pastor
New Birth Cathedral
Lithonia, Georgia

If there is a measure of truth to the old saying "timing is everything" then Earl Pitts & Craig Hills' present literary endeavor is going to be greatly blessed by God and eagerly received by Christians everywhere.

This book is right on time! It is undoubtedly the finest study I have ever seen on the basic principles of personal Kingdom-based finances. It is "must reading" for people who want to bless God and others with the way they steward their lives and finances.

Dennis Peacocke
REBUILD
Santa Rosa California

Having money may or may not be important to you, but learning how to handle what you do have must become important. Money does not come with an instruction manual and everyone has an opinion about it. Everyday there are thousands of people worrying about money, these are good honest hardworking people. The truth is that God does not want us to worry about money, just to be a good steward of it. When our mind is focused on money problems how can we focus on our purpose, helping others.

You can't win a game if you don't know the rules. After 10 years in the financial services industry I thought I had learned all the rules about personal finance, but I discovered that there is a much bigger picture. The principles outlined in this book are not quick fix answers to those with money problems, but rather a new perspective on finance for everyone. If you are having a hard time financially you will learn how to get to the root cause of your problem, how to correct it and get on the road to financial freedom. For those who have plenty of financial resources and still feel as though their money is controlling them, this new economic philosophy on stewardship will give you peace of mind.

There are hundreds of books available on personal finance, and I have read them all and so should you, but I recommend you start with this one!

Robert Weinhardt
Personal Financial Analyst
Regional Vice President
Cambridge, Ontario, Canada

CONTENTS

x

INTRODUCTION

Over the last fifteen years our (Craig and Jan Hill) ministry has been primarily concerned with marriage and family. Someone may legitimately ask, "Why are you teaching about money and finances?" In ministering to marriages, I have found over the years that peoples' attitudes toward, and mismanagement of, money is a major source of conflict in marriages and families. If one were to go to a divorce court and listen to the issues that have divided a couple, money and finances would be right on the top of the list in most cases. As a result, I have seen a tremendous need to deal not only with the practical, but also with the spiritual aspects of handling personal finances.

In the mid 1980s I heard a series of Bible teachings on the topic of money and finances given by my friend, Earl Pitts. This teaching was absolutely unique in that it dealt with the spiritual as well as the practical aspects of finance. I had read most of the popular Christian books regarding debt and finances, but the revelation the Lord had given Earl was very unique. As I began applying these truths personally and then teaching them to others, the revelation from the Lord continued to expand in my life. Consequently, I began teaching in churches a seminar on "God's Principles of Finance" regularly. We began to see many marriages healed as the pressure of financial mismanagement was relieved. We observed many families experiencing the Lord's supernatural provision in their lives as they learned to trust Him and to do the natural things that they could do.

Over the years as Earl and I have kept in touch, we discovered that the Lord had been significantly adding revelation to both of us in this area of finances. We have felt strongly compelled that now is the time to combine the revelation that both of us have received over the last decade of teaching this material. This book has thus been birthed out of our practical experience of applying these principles to our own lives and watching the principles work in the lives of many others. It is our prayer that God bless you and use the material in this book to prepare you to be a manager over a large account of finances for the Kingdom of God!

CRAIG HILL

The subject of finances has captured our attention for many years. In the past it was addressed only in the secular arena, mainly connected with the study of economics. In the church the subject of money was often discussed, but the management of such has not been adequately taught, other than to give it to the church and to the work of God. I (Earl) grew up in the 50's. After I started to deliver newspapers, I remember my father taking me to a bank, and setting up an account there for my paper route earnings. He also gave me a set of numbered church envelopes. Each envelope had two pockets: one for tithe and the other for offerings. Dad told me that the tithe was 10% and belonged to God. The offerings were what were given at my discretion over and above the tithe.

These principles have never left me. However, I had no understanding that there was a system of finance that was governed by the Kingdom of God and totally different from the world system. In the Lord's Prayer, we say "Your Kingdom come; Your will be done as it is being done in heaven... ." When a person comes under the government of the Kingdom of God, his or her finances will manifest the nature of God as a provider. Kingdom order in any individual's finances is prosperity and freedom from debt. Debt is a lack of provision and an interruption from its source. This is a break-down in the order of the Kingdom of God in the life of a believer. I had never heard a sermon dealing with money other than "the love of money is the root of all evil." As time passed, I began to find books written by Christians on how to organize one's household finances. Most of these books brought in Biblical principles, but relied on the world system when it came to dealing with investments and various forms of riches. It was what I call a "mixdom"- mixture of Biblical, Kingdom principles with the world system of finance.

In the early 80's, my wife, Dorothy, and I, along with our children, were living at the Youth With A Mission base in Cambridge, Ontario, Canada. A local pastor called me and asked if I would come and share on finances with his congregation. Their church had many young people and married couples who needed teaching in the area of finances. As I prayed about this invitation, I sensed a release from the Lord to accept, and therefore, phoned the pastor back to say that I would be glad to come and share in the church on finances. I was shocked to discover that he wanted me to speak at his main Sunday morning service. I had always felt that this type of subject should be covered on a Wednesday evening or Saturday meeting! The Pastor insisted that Sunday morning was the time.

The Lord had impressed upon me the need to study His Word in this area. Consequently, I prepared and taught for an hour what the Word of God said about finances. It was a traditional approach—tithing and giving with some helps on percentages that could be used for various expenses. On the way home after the service, I remember thinking at the time of preparation that there was much more teaching in the Bible on finances, and that I was just scratching the surface. I remember promising the Lord that I would be diligent in studying the Word on this subject.

About nine months later, after not having done anything more on this subject, our small group leaders from the YWAM base went out to eat Chinese food one evening. As usual, at the end of a meal in a western style Chinese restaurant, the server brings each diner a cookie with a message inside. My companions, when breaking open their cookies and reading the individual messages, began to laugh. However, when I opened my cookie and read the message, I did not laugh. It said, "Reaffirm your faith in financial planning and remake your budgets." I remembered the story of Balaam and the talking donkey. Now I had a cookie that was talking to me, and I was in trouble! The first thing I had to do was repent of my lack of diligence and start doing what I had told the Lord I would do. From that time on I have been in the Word of God, studying on finances, receiving revelation on the subject, and teaching regularly in this area. This book is the integration of financial understanding from teachers in the Body of Christ, through their books and audio teaching, combined with revelation by the Spirit of God in my personal study over a 16-year period. I have been asked over the years to write a book on the subject, but never felt in my spirit that the timing was right, because there was new understanding coming continually. Many times, even during a seminar, the Lord would show me new things and insights in the financial realm.

In the last two years, Craig Hill and I have been discussing the need for this book. Craig has been teaching this material for over 10 years. As we talked about the possibilities of co-authoring the book, we felt that by using this material we could merge two streams of perspectives.

EARL PITTS

PART ONE:
BALANCE IN FINANCIAL WISDOM

In beginning a discussion on personal financial management, we had to ask the question, "Does God have anything to say about money in the Bible?" Many people consider the Bible to be a book pertaining to spirituality, but not to such mundane matters as personal management of money. As we began to study this topic in the Bible, we were amazed to discover that the New Testament contains nearly ten times as many verses regarding money and finances as it does salvation and faith. **The New Testament actually contains <u>215</u> verses pertaining to faith, <u>218</u> verses pertaining to salvation, and <u>2084</u> verses dealing with the stewardship of and accountability for money and finance.** Sixteen of Jesus' thirty-eight parables deal with money.

The question comes to mind, "Why?" Was Jesus a money-grubber? Did He come to earth to collect money to support His ministry? No, of course not! Jesus was not after people's money; He was after their hearts. He told us in Matthew 6:21, "where your treasure is there shall your heart be also." Jesus simply found that many people considered their money a great treasure. He found that if He could capture their money, He could capture their hearts. We believe that the same is true today. Jesus is not after your money. He is after your heart. How we relate to money is simply indicative of the condition of our hearts.

Consequently, God has much to say to us about finances and has given us His Word to instruct us. In order for us to carry out world evangelism, it is going to take hundreds or millions of dollars. In fact, I (Earl) have heard an estimate of 2 ½ billion US dollars being needed to preach the Gospel throughout the whole world. Christians are waiting for Jesus to return to earth. Some were expecting the end of the world at the turn of the millennium. However, the Word is very clear about when this will happen. Jesus, Himself, told us that when the Gospel of the Kingdom is preached as a witness to every people group, every ethnos, every nation, then the end shall come (Matthew 24:14). Perhaps this is similar to the instruction a primary school teacher might have given us as children when we had to remain at school in order to complete an unfinished assignment. "When you are finished with your assignment, you may go home." Many want to go home without finishing the assignment.

The mandate, of course, is for us to go and preach the Gospel in the whole world. It is going to take finances to accomplish this task.

When we have finances, we can force the world system to do the work of the Kingdom of God. With finances we can buy television time and airplane tickets. We can print Bibles. We can go, preach, and make disciples. We can proclaim the Gospel of Jesus Christ. God has left us in the world after we were born again, in order to tell others about Jesus. He didn't take us immediately to heaven. His plan is to have a vast family of men and women, boys and girls, of every tongue, every tribe, and every nation with whom He will spend eternity. He left us here and said, "Go and preach My Gospel." It is going to take many people and much resource, which includes money, in order for that to take place.

One woman involved in full-time Christian ministry was confronted about receiving money for the ministry. She was told, "You should not be requesting money from people who are receiving your Bible teaching. Jesus said the gospel is freely given. 'Freely you have received. Freely give.'" This wise Christian leader responded by saying, "Obviously you have never tried to take the gospel to anyone. We have not yet convinced the airlines, television stations, print shops, and car dealerships that the Master has need of their resources, and they should freely give of their goods and services to be used in proclaiming the gospel."

When we talk about finances, it is important to distinguish between the management of personal finances and corporate finances. The scope of this book is limited to dealing with personal finances. Managing corporate or business finance in the Kingdom of God is another highly important topic to be addressed, but will not be covered in the present work. The first step toward managing a Kingdom-oriented business is to bring our personal finances into biblical order.

I (Earl) ran across a recent statistic citing the fact that 80 % of North American Christian homes have some type of financial distress, ranging from mild to serious. A primary issue cited in 50% of divorces in America today has to do with finances. Relationships have broken because of the mismanagement of finances, the lack of agreement over the usage of finances, or the mishandling of debt. In reality, the life of every single person is greatly impacted by his or her relationship to finances.

SPIRIT AND TRUTH

When Jesus was talking to the woman at the well in John chapter 4, He told her, *"God is Spirit, and those who worship Him must worship in spirit and truth."* In everything we do, it is essential that we keep a balance between spirit and truth. Everything we do as believers should be a part of our worship unto God. Thus, as we enter into discussion about our relationship to money and finances, we want to endeavor throughout this book to keep a continual balance between spirit and truth. What do we mean by this?

The truth side primarily has to do with natural, non-optional principles of life; while the spirit side has to do with relating to the spirit realm. We need to constantly live in compliance with both spirit and truth. For example, understanding and obeying the principle of gravity would pertain to the truth side. One would create many problems for oneself in life if he/she did not understand or refused to abide by the principle of gravity.

Or for example, when flying an airplane, one should understand and abide by the principles of aerodynamics. Violation of these principles can readily result in death or serious injury. However, one would also want to be led by the Holy Spirit regarding where and when to fly an airplane. It would be equally dangerous while flying either to violate a basic aerodynamic principle or to miss the specific direction of the Holy Spirit. This same balance is essential to be kept when dealing with personal finances.

On both the spirit and the truth side of the balance we want to operate in faith. All that we do must be done in faith. Apostle Paul tells us in Romans 14:23 that *"whatever is not of faith is sin."* So, how do we walk in faith regarding basic financial principles (the truth side)? We find a key to this in a parable Jesus told his disciples in Luke 17. Jesus shared this parable in response to His disciples' request to increase their faith.

LUKE 17

6   *So the Lord said, "If you have faith as a mustard seed, you can say to this mulberry tree, 'Be pulled up by the roots and be planted in the sea,' and it would obey you.*

7   *And which of you having a servant plowing or tending sheep, will say to him when he has come in from the field, 'Come at once and sit down to eat?'*

8   *But will he not rather say to him, 'Prepare something for my supper, and gird yourself and serve me till I have eaten and drunk, and afterward you will eat and drink?'*

9   *Does he thank that servant because he did the things that were commanded him? I think not.*

10 *So likewise you, when you have done all those things which you are commanded, say, 'We are unprofitable servants. We have done what was our duty to do.'"(NKJV)*

At first glance, many people will look at this and wonder, "What on earth does this have to do with faith?" First of all, faith needs to be seen as a seed. The apostles wanted increase in their faith. A seed is for planting so increase will come as it grows. As we abide in God's Word, live in it, let it mold our thinking, faith will grow and develop in our hearts. Jesus is telling His disciples here that faith comes through obedience and accountability. Faith is increased when a servant simply does that which he is told to do. Faith comes through recognizing our position as servants, and through becoming obedient to the Master's instructions already given to us in the Word of God.

We find many people who are believing God for financial increase and multiplication, but are regularly violating biblical financial principles. You may be a mighty man or woman of faith, but it would still be unwise for you to violate the law of gravity by stepping off tall cliffs and buildings. In the financial realm, you cannot regularly violate basic, financial principles and expect that by "faith" God will bring deliverance, increase and multiplication. Faith, on the truth side, comes through obedience to basic life principles.

In the chart on page 10, you will see listed on the truth side seven basic financial building blocks. These basic principles are similar to the law of gravity and cannot be violated without consequence. Violation results in turmoil, stress, financial pressure, poverty and often disaster. Obedience as a servant to these basic instructions will build faith, and produce security, peace and prosperity.

Through the course of this book, we will examine in more detail each of these seven basic principles pertaining to the management of personal finances. We will see that these building blocks must be put in place sequentially. Many Christians have become angry with God or with Bible teachers by attempting to operate in the principles of sowing and reaping (Building Block #7) when they have not yet established in their lives Building Blocks one through six. Such people then feel either deceived by Bible teachers or abandoned by God. In most cases neither is true. They have simply attempted to build a financial house with no foundation or frame structure. Many people are looking for a "quick fix" to their financial problems rather then being willing to first build a strong foundation and frame structure.

On the other hand, some have focused only on the truth side of the equation. Such people concentrate only on principles of sound financial management. However, one must also be attentive to the spirit side of the equation. We have found many people who understand correct biblical principles of financial management, but seem to have an inability to practically implement that which they know. Often this is due to a lack of understanding of the spirit side of the equation. There is literally a battle taking place in the spirit realm over our lives and financial decisions (Ephesians 6:12).

I (Craig) perceive the spirit realm to be likened to the realm in which television waves operate. Probably in the place in which you now are reading this, TV waves are present. You have no perceptive apparatus by which you could see the picture or hear the sound. However, just because you cannot perceive television waves does not mean that they do not exist. Television waves are not just a concept or an idea, but rather are a physical reality.

So it is in the spirit realm. You may have little perceptive ability to experience the spirit realm in which God, angels, demons and Satan operate. However, this does not mean that these spirit beings do not exist, or that they do not influence your life. They most certainly do, and it would behoove you to become aware of their influence upon your life and circumstances, if you are not already so aware. These influences hinder many people from being able to practically implement the truth they know.

On the spirit side of the equation we also want to recognize that it is important to be led by the Holy Spirit in all that we do financially. For example, we may recognize the basic principle of managing our finances through a budget. However, we also want to be led by the Holy Spirit as to what items are to be included in that budget. God really does have an opinion on everything pertaining to our lives. We may recognize basic principles of giving, saving or investing. Again we want to be led specifically by the Holy Spirit in the when, where, why, and how much pertaining to our giving, saving, and investing. Being led by the Holy Spirit can make a tremendous difference in the financial outcome of such activities.

In considering the spirit side of the equation, again we want to operate in faith. Apostle Paul tells us in Romans 10:17 (NKJV), *"So then faith comes by hearing and hearing by the Word of God."* There are two Greek words translated in English as 'word.' 'Logos' is used when the written word or collective sayings of God are being referred to. The second Greek word is 'rhema' which refers to the spoken word: God speaking His Word to our hearts; the voice of the Spirit putting emphasis on His written Word; God speaking His Word to our spirit. When this happens the potential for faith to arise in our hearts takes place. When we meditate on the Word of God (logos), and hearing God speak His Word (rhema), faith comes! (By the way, faith in someone else comes when we hear someone else's word and receive it.) Thus as we meditate upon specific promises that God has given us in His Word and allow God to confirm this Word to us, faith arises in our hearts toward God for the fulfillment of these promises in our lives.

In looking at the chart on the next page, we can see that on the spirit side we must recognize that everything we have comes to us as a gift from God. Anything you have ever received in your life from God, you received by His grace. Nothing came to you as a result of your works. All through life there is always a tension between relating to God on the basis of human works as opposed to relating to Him on the basis of His grace. Most people need to make a major paradigm shift in the area of receiving provision as a gift from God by His grace, rather than as something deserved or earned. We will have much more to say about this in a later section.

We see in the scripture in 2 Corinthians 9:8 that God is able to make all grace abound. He is not obligated. He is able. He does so because He loves us, but not because He has to.

When we combine both aspects of spirit and truth, we see that faith will be developed in us both through hearing and meditating on the Word of God and through obedience to establish the basic building blocks in our lives. As we do our part to establish these building blocks and receive God's grace, then God does His part in making all grace come to us in abundance to meet every need!

Let's now look at the following chart that outlines this balance between spirit and truth.

JOHN 4:23-24

SPIRIT	TRUTH
Faith *Romans 10:17* Word	Faith *Luke 17:5-10* Obedience
GRACE	**BUILDING BLOCKS**
2 CORINTHIANS 9:8	**1. RECOGNIZE AND RENOUNCE THE SPIRIT OF MAMMON**
And God is able to make all grace (every favor and earthly blessing) come to you in abundance, so that you may always and under all circumstances and whatever the need, be self sufficient, possessing enough to require no aid or support and furnished in abundance for every good work and charitable donation. (Amplified)	(Heart allegiance goes to God alone)
	2. ESTABLISH SPARROW FAITH
	(God is my source)
	3. ESTABLISH THE TITHE
	(Be a tither rather than just tithing)
	4. BECOME GOD'S MANAGER
	(Become accountable to God for administration of present resources)
	5. CLOSE THE CIRCLE
	(How much is enough?)
	6. STEP UP TO YOUR DEBT
	(Acknowledge and properly deal with all debt)
	7. BECOME A FINANCIAL EUNUCH
	(Manage the overflow for the Lord)

< **HUMILITY**

As we consider the above chart, we notice that we cross over from the truth side to the spirit side in humility. The reason we say this is that some people have viewed God as a computer or a machine. If they honor the principles, then they feel that they have a right to demand that God meet their need. No, God is not a machine. He is a person and should be related to in humility as we would relate to any other person. What father would like to have his children demand that he do thus and such because they had done what he said? No, it is his pleasure to provide for his children, but it hurts his heart to have his children demand that he perform. Thus, God does not <u>have</u> <u>to</u> do anything. He is a person and chooses to provide for us because he loves us.

As Jesus brought out in the parable in Luke 17, even after we have done everything required, we still have nothing with which to demand that God do anything. He is the master and we are the servants. The servant never comes to the master to demand anything, even when he has done all that the master required. Thus, even when we have adhered to all the truthside principles, we still cross over onto the spirit side in humility as servants. We are not demanding anything of God, but rather are receiving of His provision for us by His grace and managing the overflow He passes through us as administrators of His account, not possessors of our own accounts.

Through the course of this book, we will be looking at the seven foundational principles listed in the preceding chart. Each time we come to a new principle, we will repeat the chart, so as to remember to always keep the balance between spirit and truth. Let us now move on to talk about the spiritual power behind money and how it influences believers.

CHAPTER 1
THE POWER BEHIND MONEY
(THE MAMMON FACTOR)

MATTHEW 6

24 "No one can serve two masters; for either he will hate the one and love the other, or else he will be loyal to the one and despise the other. You cannot serve God and Mammon."
(NKJV)

This peculiar saying spoken by Jesus Christ about two thousand years ago has been a source of guilt, controversy, and contention for believers in Jesus for centuries. What did Jesus mean by saying, "You cannot serve God and Mammon?" What on earth is "Mammon?" It is frequently used as if it were just another word for money. Is this correct? Some English translations of the Bible even substitute the word money for the word Mammon used in the above-quoted passage. Does this word have another meaning of which we are unaware? If I truly want to serve God, does this mean that I should then avoid all contact with or possession of money? These are all questions, which have passed through the minds of most readers of the New Testament.

Let's begin by talking about the meaning of the above-quoted passage in Matthew 6. To what is Jesus referring when He uses the word "Mammon?" Firstly, it is important to see that whatever Mammon is, Jesus places it in a position that is diametrically opposed to God. It is anti-God. Whatever Mammon is competes with God to be served. When He said that the two, God and Mammon, could not both be served, Jesus was not speaking about a prohibition against such, but rather an impossibility of doing such. Jesus was not stating, "It would be wrong to try to serve both God and Mammon," but rather, "It is impossible to serve both God and Mammon." God and Mammon are opposites, and thus cannot both be served at the same time. Serving one categorically precludes serving the other. Thus, either God or Mammon can only be served exclusively. In order to truly serve God, one must totally renounce Mammon and have nothing at all to do with it.

Now, if "Mammon" is synonymous with "money," then the obvious conclusion is that the Christian believer should totally renounce and have nothing to do with money. People in past centuries, and some even today have believed this and thus have taken a vow of poverty and avoided all contact with money in an attempt to be wholly devoted to God. However, even taking a vow of poverty does not necessarily free one from greed or the fear of lack of provision. I do not believe that Jesus' reference to Mammon is synonymous with money.

Jesus used this ancient Aramaic word, "Mammon" to denote an entity that exists in the heavenly realm which people had worshipped as their god of finance. Every culture and religion has a name for a deity that they worship. In the Hindu religion, it is the god 'Devali.' The Buddhists have several gods to whom they make burnt offerings of paper-like money. Thus, the Mammon entity could best be described from Ephesians 6:12, where Paul states we are not wrestling with flesh and blood but against principalities and powers... in the heavenly sphere or spiritual realm. Mammon fits the category of a power in this realm that influences the hearts of mankind to love and serve money in the physical realm. It is very likely that Jesus was referring to such a god when He used this phrase in Matthew 6.

Frequently throughout their history, the Israelites had wanted to worship both the gods of the peoples in whose land they had dwelt, as well as Jehovah God. Joshua had called the people to forsake trying to serve both the false gods of the Amorites and Jehovah, but rather to choose whom they would serve, for to serve both was a choice against Jehovah (Joshua 24:15-28). I believe that Jesus here in Matthew 6 is telling His disciples that they cannot serve both the false god of finance, Mammon, and Jehovah God. They must choose. We would have readily understood had Jesus said, "You have heard of these other false gods." Most people, however, have been unfamiliar with Mammon.

What is the nature of these false gods who were worshipped by various Canaanite peoples? Were these just human-created idols? We don't think so. We believe that each of these idolatrous gods were actually demonic princes in Satan's kingdom, who were able to deceive peoples into worshipping them. Thus, Baal, Asheroth, Chemosh, Molech, Dagon, Mammon, etc. were not just human-created idols, but rather were demonic spirits, worshipped by people. Are these spirits still alive and operative today? We believe that they most certainly are. Thus, the demonic spirit behind Mammon is still operative and demanding worship, influence, and control of peoples' lives to love and trust money today even as it was in the days of Jesus' life on earth.

When Jesus stated that you cannot serve both God and Mammon, it appears that He was contrasting two spiritual entities. The word 'cannot' does not mean illegal, but rather impossible! In reality, money is impotent and has no power. God has power. The spirit of Mammon has power. Money has no power. Thus, the true power behind financial provision in your life will either be God or the spirit of Mammon, depending on whom you choose to serve. Most people, including Christians believe that the real power is in money. Therefore, until you realize the impotence of money, you will never be free from its pursuit, nor from the influence and dominion of the spirit of behind it.

THE INTENT OF THE SPIRIT OF MAMMON

JOHN 4:23-24

SPIRIT	TRUTH
Faith *Romans 10:17* Word	Faith *Luke 17:5-10* Obedience
GRACE	**BUILDING BLOCKS**
2 CORINTHIANS 9:8	**1. RECOGNIZE AND RENOUNCE THE SPIRIT OF MAMMON**
And God is able to make all grace (every favor and earthly blessing) come to you in abundance, so that you may always and under all circumstances and whatever the need, be self sufficient, possessing enough to require no aid or support and furnished in abundance for every good work and charitable donation. (Amplified)	(Heart allegiance goes to God alone)

Let us consider the purpose of this demonic entity called Mammon. Firstly, we know that any spirit operative in Satan's kingdom desires to turn the hearts of people away from God. We believe that the primary purpose of the spirit of Mammon is to obtain from people their worship, love, affection, loyalty, service. It operates through fear. Mammon loves to hear us refer to money, especially the US currency as the Almighty Dollar. In Matthew 6:24 and Luke 16:13, Jesus identifies the conflict of love, loyalty and service between God and Mammon. He said that if you love one, you will hate the other. If you are loyal to one, you will despise the other, and if you serve one, you cannot serve the other. So the purpose of Mammon is to get you to be loyal to, love and serve him, so that by default you will hate, despise, and not serve God. As Joshua called the children of Israel to attention: "Choose this day Whom you will serve" (Joshua 24:15), so the Lord poses the same question to us today.

As with all demonic entities, the primary assault is not direct, but rather operates in a cloaked manner through deception. If Mammon were to directly appear to any Christian or even unbeliever, reveal his identity and demand loyalty, love and service, very few would voluntarily submit to him. Thus, the primary tactic of Mammon is to entice people to serve him without realizing that they are doing so. He does this through propagating lies that are widely believed in the heart by most people to be truth. We believe that the paramount lie spread by the spirit of Mammon is that money contains inherent power. Mammon entices people to ascribe sacred power to money. A person who has much money is thought to be very powerful, while a person with little money is impotent. Value is ascribed to people based on net worth of money. This fact is also true about currency in a country. When a country's money is stable, we consider the country to be powerful.

Mammon entices people to place disproportionate value on money. When people believe that money has power, they are tempted to love money. This love of money then gives rise to many other forms of wickedness.

1 TIMOTHY 6

10 *For the love of money is a root of all kinds of evil, for some have strayed from the faith in their greediness, and pierced themselves through with many sorrows. (NKJV)*

Christians who believe the lie that money has power allow their travel and movements to be governed by money, rather than by God. Such ones fear the lack of money, consult their checkbook rather than God in their giving of offerings, and busy themselves with all sorts of schemes promising to deliver money. The truth is that money has no power. It is simply an amoral, impotent object, to which the spirit of Mammon ascribes great power and through which he attempts to control the lives of people.

A corollary lie, believed by many, is that the source of one's provision is his employer, spouse, investments or other channel through which money is supplied. The truth, of course, is that the power is in God, not money, and that He is the source of provision. Thus, for the believer, there is a conflict of service and love. If one loves money, then by default he is not loving God. If one empowers money to govern choices in his life, he has without realizing it, empowered the spirit of Mammon to rule his life. God may speak to him to go to a certain place, give to a certain ministry or do a certain thing and he will say to God, "I can't, because I don't have enough money." Now God is not the source, but money is the source. If you simply ask most people the question, "For what purpose do you work," they will answer, "I am working for money." Money thus is the goal, or the real source of power. **Money was never intended to by my master, but rather to be my servant.**

The key issue here is, "Who is my source?" The spirit of Mammon will continually attempt to convince us that the real power for life is in money and the channel through which it comes is my source. Thus, if I have accepted in my heart that my employer or, my husband, my investments or the economy is my source, without realizing it, I have become a slave to the spirit of Mammon.

The master/slave relationship is thus perverted. When God is my source, then money becomes my slave to be pressed into service for the Kingdom of God. A slave is accountable to its master. We direct its activity and know where it is at all times. However, when money is my source, then I become the slave of Mammon doing whatever I perceive is necessary to get money. In other words, the end and means are reversed. Money should rightly be a means by which to serve God, who is the end or the goal. When money is empowered as a source of life then God becomes the means by which Christians hope to get money. This is many times a very subtle distinction.

I (Craig) have often been present in churches in which an offering is being taken and have felt my spirit reacting negatively to something about how the offering was being taken. For years I could not identify the problem, but I just felt inside that something was wrong. Finally I was able in recent years to identify that the problem is that the offering was being motivated by the spirit of Mammon rather than by the Spirit of God. The end and means had been reversed. Rather than using money to serve God, people were being encouraged to use God to get money.

The offering was taken something like this. (We often speak of "taking an offering," while receiving an offering would embody more of a Kingdom mentality.) Lack of money was first identified as a prevailing need for many people. Next it was brought out in scripture that lack and poverty was not God's will. The biblical principle of sowing and reaping was then presented from Mark 4 or other such passages. The person taking the offering would then let people know that the way to get their needs met was to sow seed (money) into the offering and that God would then return 30-, 60- or 100-fold. Now what is wrong with this?

It is true that poverty and lack are not God's will for His people. He does want to provide for His people, and it is His will to bless people. The biblical principle of sowing and reaping, does indeed, apply to money. God does want to multiply financial seed many-fold. So what is the problem? The problem, of course, is the reversal of the master/slave, end/means relationship. This approach empowers money as the goal. "You don't have enough money. We are going to use God and God's principles to get you money. When you have money, then you will be OK." NO! God is not the servant to get you money. Money is your servant to expand the Kingdom. God is your Master. You are His steward called to manage money under His direction.

The truth then is that God is meant to be the master and money is meant to be our slave to expand the Kingdom of God. We are to use money to serve God, not use God to get money. If God is truly my source, then my employer, or investments, or bank account, or husband is merely the channel through whom my current provision comes from God. Thus, if I receive news that my job will terminate or the economy fails, I am not terrorized by fear of lack of provision, as the source (God) is still the same. He is simply changing the channel of my provision. **If God is my source, then money becomes my slave with which to serve the Kingdom. If money is my source, then God will not be my slave to get me money.** Thus, God has power and Mammon has power, but money has no power. Money will either be my slave or my master depending on whether I am serving God or the spirit of Mammon.

In working for the IBM Corporation for 19 years, I (Earl) had to come to the realization that IBM was not my source. I could not serve (be in the employment of) two masters. I had to settle the issue that God was my source (employer) and that He had seconded me to give my time to IBM and He delegated IBM to release my salary. What a place of peace! Now when I left IBM, God was still my source and He had ways to flow money to me through different channels.

At this point, you may want to reflect on your personal situation. We live in a time where many people are being laid off, forced out of their jobs because of downsizing and cost-cutting by corporations. Mammon wants to work in fear in the lives of people. However when the employer issue is settled, i.e., God being your employer, then fear has no place. Faith in God as your source and seeking Him for the place of your next assignment become the proper response.

Control by the spirit of Mammon is certainly not relegated to the realm of the poor. Mammon also governs many people who have accumulated much money. Their money is the focus and source of life to them and they will go to great lengths to protect their money and to accumulate more of it. Oftentimes Mammon grips the rich with a fear of losing what they have and likewise grips the poor with a fear of lack of provision.

PROVERBS 30

7 *Two things I request of You (Deprive me not before I die):*

8 *Remove falsehood and lies far from me; Give me neither poverty nor riches-, Feed me with the food allotted to me;*

9 *Lest I be full and deny You, and say, 'Who is the Lord?' Or lest I be poor and steal and profane the name of my God. (NKJV)*

MAMMON COUPLES WITH INIQUITY

As we will see in the following scriptural example, Mammon is a driving, compelling force in the lives of both Christians and non-Christians alike. Many times the spirit of Mammon seeks out and couples with areas of iniquity already at work in a person's life. When this is the case, the deception this spirit brings can be even deeper and more compelling than otherwise. Let us consider a blatant example from scripture of the influence of the spirit of Mammon coupled with iniquity in the life of a believer.

ACTS 8

9   But there was a man named Simon who had formerly practiced magic arts in the city to the utter amazement of the Samaritan nation, claiming that he himself was an extraordinary and distinguished person.

10 They all paid earnest attention to him, from the least to the greatest, saying, This man is that exhibition of the power of God which is called the Great.

11 And they were attentive and made much of him, because for a long time he had amazed and bewildered and dazzled them with his skill in magic arts.

12 But when they believed the good news [the Gospel] about the Kingdom of God and the name of Jesus Christ, the Messiah, as Philip preached it, they were baptized, both men and women.

13 Even Simon himself believed...and after being baptized devoted himself constantly to him. And seeing signs and miracles of great power which were being performed, he was utterly amazed. (Amplified)

Here we see that Simon becomes a believer and was baptized. His desire was to follow the Lord as he followed Phillip. Then comes the test. In verses 14 to 17, we find that Peter and John come down from Jerusalem and pray for and lay hands on the people who have believed and been baptized to receive the Holy Spirit.

ACTS 8

18 *However, when Simon saw that the Spirit was imparted through the laying on of the apostles' hands, he brought money and offered it to them,*

19 *Saying, Grant me also this power and authority, in order that any one on whom I place my hands may receive the Holy Spirit.*

20 *But Peter said to him, Destruction overtake your money and you, because you imagined you could obtain the [free] gift of God with money!*

21 *You have neither part nor lot in this matter, for your heart is all wrong in God's sight— [it is] not straight forward or right or true before God. (Amplified)*

Notice that Peter is confronting the spirit of Mammon, as it influences Simon's heart. There is a conflict in kingdoms. Mammon wants to control and have power and authority through money, buying and selling, while the Kingdom of God operates through giving and receiving. Peter promptly pin-points the problem. Simon is a believer and was baptized, but there is something wrong with his heart! The Mammon spirit has not been dealt with and it had a hold on his soul and had captured his emotions. When money is involved, there are many times, high emotions. Have you ever noticed in some families when there is a 'discussion' about money or specifically over the will of a deceased person, that there can be a huge release of emotions? The Mammon spirit in such a situation is controlling the souls of people through their emotions.

ACTS 8

22 *So repent of this depravity and wickedness of yours, and pray to the Lord that, if possible, this contriving thought and purpose of your heart may be removed and disregarded and forgiven you.*

23 For I see that you are in the gall of bitterness and a bond forged by iniquity [to fetter souls]. (Amplified)

Peter has received a word of knowledge from the Lord and makes an incredible statement that Simon is strongly poisoned by bitterness. We know that bitterness is a condition of the emotions. So when Peter stated that his heart is all wrong in God's sight, he is not saying he was not 'born again' in his spirit, but simply that there were issues of the emotions (heart in this case) that needed to be dealt with. Upon reading this, you may be asking yourself, "What has that got to do with simply asking how much money would it take to buy this power?" Simon has obviously purchased magic skills from people before to add to his repertoire of magic arts. The answer to this question is found in the word INIQUITY. The King James version of verse 23 states, ... "and in the bond of iniquity." Many other translations equate this with sin, with words such as 'captive to sin,' the chains of sin,' or 'prisoner of sin.' The word in the Greek is *'adikia'* which denotes unrighteousness. This word is the opposite of righteousness, which constitutes a quality found in the Kingdom of God ("righteousness, peace and joy in the Holy Spirit," Romans 14:17). The Greek word also means wickedness, lawlessness, rebellion, and transgression. Going deeper into the understanding, we find that there is a mystery of iniquity (2 Thessalonians 2:7) that is at work in the world.

EZEKIEL 28

15 You were blameless in your ways from the day you were created until iniquity and guilt were found in you. (Amplified)

Most scholars feel this refers to Lucifer in his state in heaven before the fall. So when Satan appeared in the garden to tempt Eve, the fall of mankind involved more that just the sin (choice to disobey— miss the mark, fall short) but that iniquity was transmitted to mankind, the iniquity of Satan himself. It is a driving force that influences the heart of mankind to disobey and choose sin. We see the willfulness of the iniquity even in little children in their early acts of rebellion.

So there is a difference between iniquity and sin. We need to have understanding of this distinction, then we can see that there is a propensity toward certain types of sin that can be transmitted through the fathers to the children for up to four generations.

DEUTERONOMY 5

9   *You shall not bow down yourself to them or serve them: for I the Lord you God am a jealous God, visiting the iniquities of the fathers upon the children to the third and fourth generation of those who hate me,*

10   *and showing mercy and steadfast love to thousands and to a thousand generations of those who love me and keep my commandments. (Amplified)*

(See also Exodus 34:7b, and Numbers 14:18b.) Again, we are talking about iniquity, not sin. Every person is responsible for his/her own sin; however, what is passed down is the bent towards, the propensity towards, a driving force in a person that influences to the point of overwhelming a person to commit a particular sin. It is a compulsion or an addiction. We see this in families, where the things that God hates such as divorce, or alcoholism will appear in generation after generation in a family tree. The iniquity has passed down generationally and has never been dealt with. Most frequently, the iniquity is the driving force in generational curses such as substance abuse, sexual immorality, mental illness, suicide, uncontrollable anger and addictions of all sorts. Now if the iniquity is never dealt with, a person can become what Jesus referred to as a worker of iniquity.

MATTHEW 7

23   *And I will profess unto them, I never knew you, depart from me, you workers of iniquity. (NKJV)*

The Psalmist refers many times to workers of iniquity.

PSALM 28

3   Drag me not away with the wicked, with the workers of iniquity, who speak peace with their neighbors, but malice and mischief are in their hearts. (Amplified)

PSALM 36

1   Transgression (like an oracle) speaks to the wicked deep in his heart. There is no fear or dread of God before his eyes.

2   For he flatters and deceives himself in his own eyes, that his iniquity will not be found out and be hated.

12 There the workers of iniquity fall and lie prostrate: they are thrust down, and shall not be able to rise. (Amplified)

A worker of iniquity would be a person who knows there is a driving force in his life and is unwilling to deal with it. He/she resists being under authority and no one can speak into his/her life. This may be due to fear of the of loss of ministry or the fear of exposure. However, if it is not dealt with, we find the consequences of iniquity stated in Ezekiel 18:30.

EZEKIEL 18

30 Therefore I will judge you, O house of Israel, every one according to his ways, says the Lord God. Repent and turn from all your transgressions, lest your iniquity be your ruin and so shall they not be a stumbling block to you. (NKJV)

We see examples of this in the lives of many men and women who started out with right motives, but their iniquities brought them down.

PSALM 66

*18   If I regard iniquity in my heart, the Lord will not hear me.
(Amplified)*

How is all this relevant to the subject of Mammon and money?
We find in Luke 16 that Jesus ties Mammon to iniquity.

LUKE 16

*10   Therefore if ye have not been faithful in the unrighteous
Mammon, who will commit to your trust the true riches?
(NKJV)*

The word translated unrighteous is the Greek word *adikia*—
iniquity. Thus in this passage Mammon is equated with iniquity,
Mammon of iniquity. This helps explains why the love of money is
such a driving force in the lives of many people. Not only is there a
demonic spirit influencing them, but there is also a driving force
within them. Today people kill, steal, and destroy other people, things
and wealth for money. It is a consuming, driving force in all cultures
and peoples in the earth and is iniquity driven.

A spirit of poverty can be a generational curse on a person. It is
tied to iniquity and can be passed down in families. It will hold
people in bondage and hinder the flow of finances in their lives until
dealt with through repentance and cleansing by the Blood of Jesus.

Let's consider some other aspects of iniquity in order to enlarge
our understanding. Iniquity strongly affected the life of the prophet
Balaam.

2 PETER 2

*15   Forsaking the straight road they have gone astray; they have
followed the way of Balaam, [the son] of Beor, <u>who loved
the reward of wickedness</u> (Gr. adikia -iniquity).*

16 But he was rebuked for his own transgression (Gr. paranomia— another word for iniquity) when a dumb beast of burden spoke with human voice and checked the prophet's madness. (Amplified)

Here we are told of Balaam's iniquity. When we go to the story in Numbers 22, we find that there was a love of money involved in his life as he was being paid to prophesy a curse over Israel. Peter indicates by using the Greek word *adikia* that Balaam's going astray was iniquity driven.

ISAIAH 43

24 You have not bought Me sweet cane with money, or satiated Me with the fat of your sacrifices, but you have only burdened Me with your sins, you have wearied Me with your iniquities. (Amplified)

The Lord wants us to take an active part in dealing with patterns of iniquity which we have not able to overcome. When we see such repeated patterns or driving forces in our lives, it is critical that we take an active part in seeking God for revelation of the root of iniquity, so that God might grant us repentance and removal of the iniquity. However, just as Peter in Acts 8:23 told Simon that the iniquity was locked into bitterness, the iniquity in your life may be rooted in some other area. The iniquity may, however, manifest itself, as it did in Simon's life, in the love of money. Simon's love of money was demonstrated in his desire to use money to attempt to purchase power and authority over the lives of other people.

Here is an interesting side note dealing with the hording of US currency in notes of larger denomination. The New York Times quoted a report issued by the Federal Reserve Bank of Los Angeles on May 22, 1994,[1] listing the total volume of US currency in circulation by denomination. The report stated that in 1992 the total

---

[1] The New York Times, Times National Section, May 22, 1994, page 12.

currency in circulation was $292 billion, which is $1,143 for every man, woman and child living in the USA. In looking at the currency in circulation by denomination, we find that there are over six $100 bills in circulation for every man, woman and child in the USA. Since most law abiding citizens use checks, credit cards, or debit cards for most transactions, who is holding all these $100 bills? It turns out that the $157 billion in $100 bills represents primarily the savings and working capital of the underworld. Through this underground economy we see that the love of money is the root of all evil!

Praise God that He has not left us without answers in dealing with iniquity. In Isaiah 53 we start to see the provision God has made for us in Jesus Christ.

ISAIAH 53

5   *But He was wounded for our transgressions, He was bruised for our guilt and iniquities; the chastisement needful to obtain peace and well-being for us was upon Him, and with the stripes that wounded Him we are healed and made whole. (Amplified)*

It is clear that Jesus died both for transgressions or sins and for iniquities. The way the prophet describes the death of Jesus is by wounding and bruising. The wounding of Jesus is attributed to our transgressions, while we are told that the bruising was for our iniquities. We can see through this description, that wounding is external, manifested through lacerations, piercings, and the ripping and tearing of flesh. The bruising, however, to deal with iniquity, required an internal injury resulting in bruising and subsurface bleeding. The internal bruising can be far more painful than an external cut. We understand physical bruising and how painful and hurting it can be. How much more is the bruising in the emotions, where words and actions hurt us? Apostle James talks about the tongue as a fire.

JAMES 3

6   And the tongue [is] a fire. [The tongue is a] world of
wickedness [Gr.-adikia -iniquity] set among our members,
contaminating and depraving the whole body and setting on
fire the wheel of birth -the cycle of man's nature— being
itself ignited by hell. (Amplified)

Notice that the tongue is the primary transmitter of iniquity.
Words emanating from iniquity do not just cause superficial wounds
in their recipient, but rather curse the identity, penetrating deep into
the emotions and lodging there. The iniquity is like a gall or ongoing
poison that can retain bitterness, or other sins such as in the case of
Simon. Now iniquity is like a glue or bonding agent that will attract
and retain anything else that is of iniquity.

ACTS 8

23   For I see that you are in the gall of bitterness, a bond forged
by iniquity [to fetter souls]. (Amplified)

So the Mammon spirit (a demonic entity which is of iniquity)
had a place to reside in the emotions of Simon through his bitterness.
This spirit was able to defile his soul with the love of money and the
deception of what he thought money could produce in his life.

We find the antidote to iniquity described in 1 John 1.

1 JOHN 1

9   If we [freely] admit that we have sinned and confess our
sins, He is faithful and just [true to His own nature and
promises] and will forgive our sins and continuously cleanse
us from all unrighteousness (Gr. adikia iniquity) everything
not in conformity to His will in purpose, thought and action.
(Amplified)

Here John tells us there is a cleansing for all iniquity. The cleansing agent is the Blood of Jesus. However, it must be applied to the iniquity just as confessing our sins (specifically) is necessary for forgiveness to be received. Peter called Simon to repent of his iniquity, or to allow his mind to be changed and renewed. He was told not to be a "worker of iniquity," but rather to deal with it. So with the Mammon spirit, we must deal with the iniquity that allows it to attach to our emotions. The fear of the lack of money, loving it and serving it and all the bondages that love of money produces have to be recognized and cleansed by the Blood of Jesus. This Blood must be applied so that true repentance will take place and the resultant sins that have been working in our lives can be confessed and forgiven. Once the iniquity and sin have been dealt with, then true freedom from the bonded Mammon spirit can be experienced.

In order to maintain our freedom from the love of money, the opposite of iniquity has to be put into effect and practiced. We find the opposite of iniquity spoken of by Apostle Paul in Romans 6.

ROMANS 6

13 Do not continue offering or yielding your bodily members [and facilities] to sin as <u>instruments (tools) of wickedness</u> (Gr.-adikia -iniquity). But offer and yield yourselves to God as though you have been raised from the dead to [perpetual] life, and your bodily members [and facilities] to God, presenting them as <u>implements of righteousness</u>.

18 And, having been set free from sin, you have become the servants of righteousness— of conformity to the divine will in thought, purpose and action.

19 I am speaking in familiar human terms, because of your natural limitations. For as you yielded your bodily members [and facilities] as servants of impurity and ever increasing lawlessness (Gr. adikia unto adikia, literally to iniquity unto iniquity), so now yield your bodily members and [facilities] once for all as servants to righteousness— right being and doing— [which leads] to sanctification. (Amplified)

Righteousness is the opposite of iniquity. The Word of God continually encourages us in righteousness.

ROMANS 6

16 *Do you not know that if you continually surrender yourselves to anyone to do his will, you are the slaves of him whom you obey, whether that be to sin, which leads to death, or to obedience which leads to righteousness— right doing and right standing with God? (Amplified)*

So we see that surrender to God and his Word leads to righteousness and will keep us free from iniquity.

ROMANS 5

21 *So that, [just] as sin has reigned in death, so grace— His unearned and undeserved favor— might reign also through righteousness (right standing with God) which issues in eternal life through Jesus Christ, the Messiah the Anointed One, our Lord. (Amplified)*

God is calling us to operate in His grace which reigns, has authority, through righteousness. God then calls us to reign.

ROMANS 5

17 *For if, because of one man's trespasses (lapse, offense) death reigned through that one, much more surely will those who receive [God's] overflowing grace and the free gift of righteousness (putting them into right standing with Himself) reign in life through the One, Jesus Christ, the Messiah, the Anointed One. (Amplified)*

Our reigning, having authority, dominion and power, comes by His righteousness as a free gift and abundance of grace. All of this has been designed by God to keep us free from iniquity. We must have a perception of ourselves as righteousness. Our focus must be upon our righteousness in Christ, not upon our iniquity in the flesh. We are the righteousness of God in Christ Jesus according to Paul in 2 Corinthians 5.

2 CORINTHIANS 5

21 *For our sake He made Christ to be sin Who knew no sin, so that in and through Him we might become the righteousness of God. (Amplified)*

The scepter of God's Kingdom is righteousness (Hebrews 1:8).

HEBREWS 1

9a *You have loved righteousness— You have delighted in integrity, virtue, uprightness of purpose, thought and action— and You have hated lawlessness (Gr.- adikia) (injustice and iniquity). (Amplified)*

JOHN 16

8 *And when He (the Holy Spirit) has come, He will convict the world of sin, and of righteousness, and of judgment:*

9 *Of sin, because they do not believe in Me;*

10 *Of righteousness, because I go to My Father and you see Me no more;*

11 *Of judgment, because the ruler of this world is judged. (NKJV)*

Most people have thought that the Holy Spirit came on the earth to convict us of all the things we are doing wrong (sin), that God is angry with us because He is righteous (righteousness), and that God will judge us if we don't stop sinning (judgment). This is just the opposite of what Jesus actually said in this scripture.

According to Jesus, the Holy Spirit has come to convict us in any area of unbelief in Jesus, of our own righteousness in Christ, and of the fact that the devil has already been judged and thus has no power in our lives. The only sin that the Holy Spirit is convicting anyone of, is that of not believing or trusting in Jesus. Whenever iniquity is operative in the life of a believer, at that moment and in that area of life, that person is not believing and trusting in Jesus. When most people become aware of iniquity, they usually begin to strive in their own determination and willpower to rid their life of that iniquity. This is why the Holy Spirit will then convict us that we have no ability to deal with iniquity by our own willpower. He will convict us that we are not believing in Jesus, and that Jesus' blood frees us, not our self effort.

The Holy Spirit is not trying to tell us all the things we did wrong. Our own hearts are busy continually telling us about all of the unrighteousness in our lives. The Holy Spirit is primarily trying to get us to believe that we are righteous in Christ. Furthermore, He didn't come to tell us that if we don't quit sinning, God will judge us, but rather that the ruler of this world (Satan) is already judged. Thus, a chief work of the Holy Spirit is to help us to accept and identify with our righteousness, which Jesus purchased for us.

MATTHEW 6

33 But seek first the Kingdom of God and His righteousness and all these things shall be added unto you. (NKJV)

Notice the double emphasis on righteousness. In Romans 14:17, the Kingdom of God is defined as righteousness, peace and joy in the Holy Spirit. Thus Matthew 6:33 could read, Seek first righteousness, peace and joy in the Holy Spirit and righteousness.... . We believe the double emphasis is to remind us that the opposite of iniquity is righteousness, God's Righteousness, which is ours through Jesus. We encourage you to study and meditate on the subject of righteousness. Develop a Righteousness consciousness!

We see then from Acts 8 that Simon needed to deal with iniquity in his soul, even though he was born again and baptized. His heart treasured money and what it could buy. Jesus wants us free from iniquity so that the Mammon spirit has no place to lodge in our emotions and keep us in bondage and slavery to loving money.

Thus, in summary, the purpose of the spirit of Mammon is to get people to empower money with sacred value, thus making money their source of well-being in life. People will then love money rather than God and fear the lack of money rather than fearing God. Here is a powerful statement that is worthy of memorization. **If God is your source, money is to be your slave with which to accomplish Kingdom work. Conversely, if money is your source, God will not be your slave to get you money!** <u>**Until you realize how impotent money really is, you will never be free from its pursuit!**</u> Let us now deal with the signs of Mammon's influence in our lives so that we can recognize any place in which the enemy may have access into our emotions through the love of money.

TEN SYMPTOMS OF MAMMON'S INFLUENCE

Most people do not recognize the influence of the spirit of Mammon in their lives. We would like to list here ten symptoms we have observed of the influence of the spirit of Mammon in a person's life. Identification of the influence of this spirit is the first step to freedom from it. Here are the ten symptoms.

1. Worry and Anxiety Over Money.

Many people carry much anxiety and fear over money. Rich people fear losing the money they have, while poor people fear never having enough money. In either case fear, worry and anxiety dominate a person's emotions.

We are told the following in Proverbs 30:7-9:

PROVERBS 30

7 *Two things I request of You (Deprive me not before I die):*

8 *Remove falsehood and lies far from me; Give me neither poverty nor riches— Feed me with the food allotted to me;*

9 *Lest I be full and deny You, and say, ' Who is the Lord?' Or lest I be poor and steal, and profane the name of my God. (Amplified)*

Sparrow Faith frees us from the focus on money as a source of provision and thereby from the anxiety and worry over it. Freedom from anxiety over money is characterized by the presence of the following three inner attitudes.

A. What I have I have received as a gift from God. I am merely a steward of that which God has entrusted to me. My needs are met by God and not by my efforts. I have no need to worry over money because all I have available to me is a gift from my Heavenly Father, Who loves me. This sets my heart free from fear and anxiety.

B. My possessions are cared for by God. When I recognize that all I have is a gift from God, then I can allow Him to retain possession, and I am merely a manager of His resources. Thus, if something is stolen or damaged, I can know that if God wants me to continue to have this item, He can replace it. Thus, I can be free from anxiety over the retention and care of possessions.

C. My possessions are available to be used by others. Because I own nothing and am only a manager of God's resources, I can make possessions or resources available to others as the Lord directs, without fear of loss or damage. As a good steward, I will instruct people on the proper use of an item so they will care for and be a good steward also.

There was an insightful article in Time Magazine under the behavior section of the February 29, 1988 issue. It was titled, the "Woes of Being Wealthy." The article spoke of the plague of anxieties that seems to afflict a growing number of the very rich. The malady is called "affleunza." Psychologists are slowly recognizing that great riches are sometimes accompanied by a wealth of crippling emotional and psychological fears. The article further states, that in families in which riches have extended through several generations, there is frequently found a chronic and pervasive terror of losing the fortunes that have given these families a sense of identity.

In Matthew 6:25-34, Jesus states five times, not to worry or have anxiety over the source of provision and states in verse 33:

MATTHEW 6

33 But seek for (aim at and strive after) first of all His Kingdom and His righteousness (His way of doing and being right), and then all these things taken together will be given you besides. (Amplified)

Focus is the primary issue. Seeking first is a preoccupation of mind and heart that seeks God and His ways. It will surely keep us from worry and anxiety over finances. In this section of Scripture, God has placed a "lie detector." If I ask people "are you seeking first the Kingdom of God and His righteousness?," many reply. "Oh yes; sure; certainly!" But as our conversation progresses, I find they start talking worry and anxiety over finances! Their talk reveals what is really in the heart and they are not seeking first the Kingdom. Seeking is a preoccupation with something, and will keep you from worry and anxiety when it is directed to the Kingdom of God.

2. Money Mismanagement. "I don't know where it went."

Many Christians have no system of record-keeping for their personal finances. As a result of this, they have no financial accountability in their lives, even to themselves. Such people could not even tell you the regular monthly amount necessary for their provision. I (Craig) have given the following analogy to many people.

Suppose that you were the manager of a multi-trillion dollar trust fund, the purpose of which was to disperse funds to Christian people who would use those funds wisely in pursuit of the Kingdom of God.

Suppose two Christian families came in to apply for an allocation of funds. The first family came to you with a past history of how money had been used and a budget for the use of the funds to be disbursed.

The second family came to you with no past history of usage of funds and no budget for the future. When you asked the husband how much money he was applying for, he told you, "A few thousand dollars." You then queried how many thousand exactly. "Oh, I don't know. Maybe seven thousand," he replied. "For what are you going to use it?" you ask. "To pay my bills." "How much are your bills each month?" you ask. "I don't know exactly," he says.

Now to which one of these two families would you rather release funds? "To the first family," they will inevitably respond. I then ask another question. If you were such a fund manager, could you with fiduciary integrity toward the owner of the fund invest money in your own family? Many times the person will hang his head in shame and answer, "No." "Why not?" I ask. "Because my situation is like that of the second family. I have no budget or record-keeping system for my finances," he answers. I then have to ask the hard question, " Do you think that God is more foolish than man? If you wouldn't even invest in you, why would God?"

I then tell this person that God really does have a multi-trillion dollar trust fund. He is even right now accepting applications. However, you need to prepare your financial record-keeping system so that you know how much money to apply for and to be able to give some accountability to the manager of the fund as to how the funds will be used.

Money mismanagement is symptomatic of not keeping any records and having no financial plan. Some have taken the attitude that since God is the source, they need to keep no records and have no plan. This will always lead to irresponsibility and money mismanagement.

3. **Consistent Financial Lack.** "I don't ever have enough money." Too much month left at the end of the money.

This problem seems to afflict both the rich and the poor alike. When I do not see myself as a manager of finances, accountable before God, then I will have no record keeping and no budget. This results in spending patterns that consistently exceed available resource. The deception of consumer debt then becomes very attractive as a short-term solution for financial lack.

If a family consistently spends 120% of the available financial resource, they will constantly perceive themselves to have a lack of necessary resource. Many people believe the lie that if they could just make more money, their financial problems would be solved. In reality, it is the way their money is spent that is the problem, not the amount that is available. If a pattern of spending 120% of available resource is established, does it really matter if there is $1,000, $10,000, or $100,000 per month available? The larger number simply generates a $20,000 per month shortfall, rather than a $200 per month shortfall for the smaller number. The more money you have monthly will make only more options available to you for spending the money.

4. "I Can't Afford It" Mentality.

If the spirit of Mammon has convinced me that money is my source and is the determining factor in my life, then I must be very careful with how I spend money. This again is a focus on money rather than on God as a source. I (Craig) remember one man I met who had done very well at creating an asset base of several million dollars. However, he was very protective of his money and had great difficulty letting go of any of it. Consequently, whenever his wife and children desired to spend money on legitimate needs and desires, they were constantly told, "we can't afford it." Again this can afflict both the rich and the poor. It is a mental stronghold, not dependent upon the financial situation.

As good stewards we have to answer the question "how much is enough?" The Mammon spirit does not want us to answer that question. It is this spirit that induces the need. God wants to work with us in answering that question. Jesus was not motivated by need. He did only what the Father told him to do, even in the face of incredible need. The devil will never cease to create needs. Therefore, if we are driven by need, guess whom we are following? Our heavenly Father knows our needs before we ask Him (Matthew 6:8b). We will be talking in a subsequent chapter about the mechanics of creating a "closed circle" or a budget that captures our Obligations, Necessities and Wants. Since the Lord desires to be in agreement with us over our finances, we will want to inquire of God as to what is to be included in this circle.

The prophet in Amos 3:3 poses the question, "Can any two walk together except they be in agreement?" I am sure that we all want the Lord to walk together with us in the area of finances. Now when we seek Him as to what should be in our circle in the Necessities and Wants area, and we obey what He tells us, then the "I can't afford it" mentality is a non-issue. If you have truly sought the Lord regarding His will and timing for you to have a particular item, then it is to be included in your circle. When you follow this strategy, the temptation from advertising to create need in your heart and mind is defeated! It is simply a temptation that can be resisted. We will teach you how to do this in the practical application later in the book.

5. Impulse Buying. Inability to resist the desire to purchase.

Many times a person will come home with a new purchase and the marriage partner will exclaim, "Why did you buy that? What do we need it for?" The answer will come, "I don't know, but I got a deal. It was cheap." Many people purchase all sorts of things that they really don't need or even want simply because it was cheap. As you walk through the shopping mall (a temple to Mammon), the spirit of Mammon is screaming out through all sorts of things, "Buy me! Buy me! I'm cheap. You'll never get this good deal again." This is a pattern established in the lives of many people who have not yet learned to be a manager of resources and allow the Holy Spirit to be the master.

I (Earl) have discovered that there are cities in the world over which the spirit of Mammon rules. Hong Kong has been one of them. I remember the first time Dorothy, my wife, and I went to Hong Kong. Before we went, we were told by a friend to take multiple empty suitcases with us, because there were so many things to buy in Hong Kong at such good prices compared to back home in Canada.

After we arrived, we had time on our schedule to take a trip downtown and began to walk through this huge emporium. I told my wife, "Look at these prices. This is incredible! Do you realize that back home the prices of these items would be five times what they are here?" We really had a struggle just walking through the store. As we began to load up a shopping basket, I felt my pulse increasing and perspiration appearing on my forehead. Anxiety was increasing and as I thought about it, I realized that the anxiety was that I might miss one of the aisles and miss out on a really good deal!

I turned to my wife and exclaimed, "Dot, something is happening to me. There is a spirit of Mammon influencing me. Let's leave this stuff for now and get a cup of tea." We sat down and began to make a list of people we wanted to bless through the purchase of items in that store. I realized that by focusing on using money to bless others through giving we would break the power of the spirit of Mammon over our minds. I then walked back into the store totally free from the anxiety and pressure I had felt before. We made our purchases for the purpose of blessing others and then left the store with peace in our hearts.

I have found that his spirit works so strongly on the mind that sometimes people are almost trampled to death trying to get into a sale. The secret is always to shop with a list of items to be purchased for your closed circle, which may include names of people you want to bless!

6. Stinginess. This is exemplified by a fear of tithing.

Some people have more fear of letting go of money than Scrooge at Christmas time. Fear of tithing or giving is always a symptom of a strong yielding to the spirit of Mammon. Stinginess is simply a fear that I won't have enough money to meet my own needs. This fear then generates a need to hold on to money. Again, this characteristic is often independent of the financial situation. Some people who handle large quantities of financial resources are very stingy. They pay their bills late and don't tithe due to the stronghold of stinginess in their minds. Other people who have very little are equally stingy. For either the rich or the poor, stinginess is a symptom of bondage to the spirit of Mammon.

It had been reported that one of the richest men in the world, who is now deceased, had a pay telephone installed in his house for his guests to use. This must be the height of stinginess.

7. Greed. This is an inordinate desire to acquire or possess.

Some people mix the definitions of covetousness and greed. What is the difference? Covetousness has to do with desiring after something that you don't have, while greed is the desire for more of what you already have. In Luke 12:16-20 Jesus tells us a story of a rich man who was continually building barns to contain more of his crops and goods. In the end, God called him a fool and told him that his trust in his possessions and not in God would cost him his soul. If you ask a wealthy man who has never closed his circle the question "How much is enough?," he will answer you, "Just a little bit more."

The world system is designed to create need. Merchants offer one item free or at a low cost and follow up with a "series" of items. "This is one of 10 or 100 that you will want to collect. Of course, you can cancel at any time," they tell you. Once you enter this system governed by the spirit of Mammon, you will have great difficulty trying to stop. Most people enter into a conversation with themselves and some type of justification process will take place. We all have experienced this at some time in our lives, in varying degrees.

8. Discontentment.

PHILIPPIANS 4

11 Not that I am implying that I was in any personal want, for I have learned how to be content (satisfied to the point where I am not disturbed or disquieted) in whatever state I am.

12 I know how to be abased and live humbly in straitened circumstances, and I know also how to enjoy plenty and live in abundance. I have learned in any and all circumstances, the secret of facing every situation, whether well-fed or going hungry, having a sufficiency and to spare or going without and being in want.

13 I have the strength for all things in Christ Who empowers me. (Amplified)

Some people can identify with Paul and say that they know what it is like to be in want. However, the key to the verses is that Paul knew HOW to live in this situation. He "knows how" to live with much or little. When we look at Paul's circumstances, we find there the times when he had little were when God told him to give away what he had. Knowing how to live with having little or much was to not be controlled by the spirit of Mammon. The key is to look to God and know He is your source in every situation and to never allow yourself to become discontent because of your circumstances.

I (Earl) wondered why Paul would find himself in such extremes: from having nothing, to plenty and living in abundance. I am sure that Paul, in obedience to the Lord, gave all that he had, thereby lending to the Lord who then repaid in an overflowing manner (Proverbs 19:17). You cannot outgive God.

9. Bondage to Debt. (Psalm 7:15; 37:21)

There is a spirit behind personal debt, which couples itself with Mammon and will hinder the flow of finances in one's life. Debt is one of the chief mechanisms used by the spirit of Mammon to keep people in bondage to itself. When the spirit of Mammon is ruling in a person's life, that person is frequently placed in financial slavery through the weight of interest owed on debt. People in bondage to the spirit of Mammon are often not able to discipline themselves to delay the personal gratification of the immediate purchase of desired items. Unplanned consumer spending is always a very strong indicator of the lordship of the spirit of Mammon in a person's life. The world system encourages personal debt through the use of credit cards. We must learn how to manage our personal debt to get out of it and stay out of it. Handling credit cards properly is a skill that can be learned.

You can release a spirit of debt over a person by how we lend money. The banks set the rules for borrowing money. The repayment is to be serviced monthly. As Christians with other Christians or family members, we want to be relational and may say "pay me back when you can!" Never do that, as it violates the principles of the world system and places the borrower under the influence of the Mammon spirit. This spirit will try to stop the flow of finances, so the debt cannot be repaid and destroy the relationship between these two people. How many people do you know that have strains in relationships with people because of lending money improperly.

In Chapter seven, we will talk more extensively on dealing with personal debt and proper borrowing that maintains relationships.

10. Exaggerated Emphasis on Money and an Overestimate of its True Power.

Often one can hear this emphasis in the language people use. When you listen to some people talk, most of what they are talking about has to do with money. They are very impressed by others who have much money. They are constantly talking about how they might make more money. There is continually a strong emphasis in their conversation on pursuing money. **However, God's plan was for money to pursue us.** We are not meant to be working to make money, but rather being available for ways to release money and make it work for us.

EPHESIANS 4

28 *Let the thief steal no more, but rather let him be industrious, making an honest living with his hands, so that he may be able to give to those in need. (Amplified)*

The reason we work is to be able to make a giving!

Money is given a very prominent place in the life of such a person, and he/she really believes that true power in life is contained in money. This person thinks that people who have lots of money are endued with great power, and people who have little money are impotent. Many governments around the world seem to think that every social problem can be solved with money. When there is a problem with drugs, crime, etc., they ask "how much money to fix the problems?" Christians often even believe, "If I just had a little more money, I could do so much more for the Kingdom." This again is an indicator that Mammon governs our ability to serve God rather than God being the source and governing our service. This sets us up to give the spirit of Mammon authority to determine our actions by simply providing or withholding money. If money is the determining factor for you to do something, then you are for sale. **If you are for sale, the devil will find your price.**

A number of years ago, Bob Mumford, a well-known Bible teacher, distributed an audio cassette to his Lifechangers constituents. The tape was called "Mammon— A Prophetic Insight." [2] Bob had listened to tapes of a financial seminar that I (Earl) had given, and the Lord had given Bob specific additional revelation in this area. I would like to give you the seven highlights that Bob shared in his taped message.

1. Wealth in any form cannot be part of my person. I am always a steward. "Owner of nothing, steward of everything."

2. The definition of "true riches" is to be conformed to His image. When we respond to Kingdom principles, these principles build in us true riches.

3. Mammon forces a trade: earthly for heavenly. This spirit says, "Serve me, and I will bless you!"

4. You cannot pursue money for its own sake. If you do, you will lose the primacy of the Kingdom of God.

5. A steward must never neglect stewardship. Handle it properly. If you appropriate it as your own, you will create trouble in your own life.

---

[2] "Lifechangers" Series, Copyright by Bob Mumford. Tape is available through Lifechangers PO Box 98088, Raleigh, N.C. 27624 Tape # A436.

6. Never suppose you can serve the Kingdom of God without your finances being at His service. We must give up our control.

7. God's love is His Nature and way to deal with us regarding the love of money.

We highly encourage you to pause here and ask the Spirit of God to reveal areas in you life in which the spirit of Mammon has influence over your mind and heart (emotions especially). Repentance is God's way of dealing with these things.

CHAPTER 2
SPARROW FAITH

JOHN 4:23-24

SPIRIT	TRUTH
Faith *Romans 10:17* **Word**	**Faith** *Luke 17:5-10* **Obedience**
GRACE	**BUILDING BLOCKS**
2 CORINTHIANS 9:8	1. RECOGNIZE AND RENOUNCE THE SPIRIT OF MAMMON
And God is able to make all grace (every favor and earthly blessing) come to you in abundance, so that you may always and under all circumstances and whatever the need, be self sufficient, possessing enough to require no aid or support and furnished in abundance for every good work and charitable donation. (Amplified)	(Heart allegiance goes to God alone)
	2. ESTABLISH SPARROW FAITH
	(God is my source)

How a Christian relates to money is an indicator of his/her understanding of God's grace. The basic, operative principle in God's economy is giving and receiving, while the basic, operative principle in the world system is buying and selling. Giving and receiving are a unilateral manifestation of grace. When you give, you expect nothing in return. Buying and selling demands an exchange. So when I take that which was designed by man for buying and selling, namely money, and freely give it with no expectation of return, I have introduced money to grace. In doing so, I have profaned the sacred properties ascribed to money and have declared to the spiritual and natural realm that Mammon is not my source.

Now when a Christian gives in an offering with an expectation of return in order to get his/her needs met, he/she is not understanding God's grace. If I (Craig) have heard it once, I have heard it taught a hundred times that if you are experiencing financial lack, the way to get your needs met is by financial sowing and reaping. This is wrong, wrong, wrong, wrong, wrong! This understanding nullifies the grace of God; places one back in the world system of exchange, and submits one's heart to be governed by the spirit of Mammon while thinking one is serving God. Further in the Matthew 6 passage, Jesus specifically taught against this idea of sowing and reaping to meet one's needs.

MATTHEW 6

24 *No one can serve two masters; for either he will hate the one and love the other, or else he will be loyal to the one and despise the other. You cannot serve God and Mammon.*

25 *Therefore I say to you, do not worry about your life, what you will eat or what you will drink; nor about your body, what you will put on. Is not life more than food and the body more than clothing?*

26 *Look at the birds of the air, <u>for they neither sow nor reap</u> nor gather into barns; yet your Heavenly Father feeds them. Are you not of more value than they? Which of you by worrying can add one cubit to his stature? So why do you worry about clothing? Consider the lilies of the field, how they grow: they neither toil nor spin; and yet I say to you that even Solomon in all his glory was not arrayed like one of these. (NKJV)*

Here we see Jesus introducing His disciples to grace, by breaking the lie that God, through sowing and reaping, will meet human needs. Jesus is making the point that God provides the basic needs of sparrows and lilies without their sowing or reaping or toiling or spinning. In other words, **their provision is not dependent upon their works**. Birds and flowers are cared for by God simply because He values them. Jesus then makes the point that you as a person are of much greater value to God than are birds and flowers. Thus, Jesus teaches that basic provision for life is made by your Heavenly Father just because He loves you. This is what I (Craig) have come to call **"Sparrow Faith."** Sparrow Faith is the initial foundation upon which all other financial operations in the Kingdom of God must be based. Without the foundation of Sparrow Faith, a basic trust that God will provide for my needs because He loves me, subsequent biblical principles of finance are easily distorted by the spirit of Mammon and used to confuse people.

You may ask, "Are you saying that financial sowing and reaping with an expectation of return is wrong?" No, not at all! Sowing and reaping is a correct biblical principle, but not to be used for getting one's needs met. The way this principle is frequently taught nullifies God's grace and makes the meeting of your needs dependent upon your works, not upon God's love.

Sparrow Faith, then, is the foundation cornerstone of Christian financial structure. This is an absolute trust and confidence and leaning of one's entire personality upon the fact that God loves me and will make provision for me. Thus, the provision which I now receive, must be understood in the context of Sparrow Faith as a gift from God, not as something due me. If I work forty hours per week for an employer, Sparrow Faith says that I am working as unto God, not unto man. The money I receive from my employer is not my due from him, but rather is provision made available to me by grace as a gift from my Father, who loves me. This fact then makes God my source of provision and my employer merely delegated as the current channel through which my provision comes.

Now with this understanding, if I hear that the company for which I work is downsizing and I may lose my employment, my heart is not terrorized by the fear of lack of provision, because my employer was not my source. The source has not changed. God's love for me has not changed. So my provision is secure. God may simply use a different channel through which to provide for my needs. Many people have thought that provision necessarily must be in the form of money. This is not true. God could provide for you a house, car, food, an airplane, whatever you need to fulfill your calling, all without money. Again, Mammon continually promotes the message that power for life is in money. God provided food for Elijah (1 Samuel 17), food, clothing and housing for Mephibosheth (2 Samuel 9), food for five thousand people through Jesus, all without money.

With this understanding, I become a manager of wealth and/or money, which comes to me as a gift by grace from my Heavenly Father. Recognizing that He is my source, money no longer controls my life. When the Lord speaks to me to give in an offering, I no longer see that as my money, which I worked hard to get, the purchasing power of which I am now relinquishing, at great sacrifice to myself. No! I see myself as a manager of a small portion of resources whether God's or from the world system over which God requires me to steward. Because my personal provision is already secure in His love, that is not jeopardized when He asks me to direct some of the resource to a particular purpose in His Kingdom. I am no longer bound to pray to my checkbook when an offering opportunity is made available ("Oh, dear checkbook, how much is in you?"), but rather I am free to pray to the Living God to find out what He wants done with this resource.

So, again Sparrow Faith is a key foundational principle. When this is not in place in a Christian's life, he will not see money as a tool with which to serve God, but rather he will see only the purchasing power of the money in exchange for goods and services which he needs. Let me give you a couple of practical examples.

I (Craig) was one time ministering in Africa among native people. Most of these people considered themselves very poor. Some were not really so poor and had quite good jobs by the standards of the economy of that particular nation. I was ministering at a leadership conference for one week. The founder of the movement of churches took an offering at each meeting of the conference and over the course of the week had received in total the equivalent of approximately forty-two U.S. dollars. The conference had cost him in direct expenses more than five times this to conduct. The church leaders attending the conference apparently saw no value in giving.

However, I had brought with me a selection of books and tapes, which I was prepared to give to these leaders. I realized, however, that they probably would not value these materials if I gave them at no cost. Therefore, I designated a nominal cost for each book or tape series. All of these materials were instantly purchased within the first two meetings. Now, it was interesting to note that these "poor" Christian leaders had no money to give in the offering, but plenty of money to buy what they desired. In other words, they did not recognize any value coming to them through giving in an offering, but recognized the immediate value of exchanging money for a book or tape series. This again is a strong symptom of bondage to the spirit of Mammon. Money has value only when it can be exchanged for something of immediate value. This attitude is not unique to rural Africa, but is also commonly found among Christians in any western country.

I remember hearing of a survey done back about 1990 regarding the usage of money among Charismatic Christians worldwide. According to my notes, this survey found that the average Charismatic Christian gave into the Kingdom $15.60 per year, or about $0.30 per week. However, the same group was found to spend $1.87 per week on Christian books, videos, cassettes, gifts, and conventions. Apparently, Charismatic Christians worldwide found far more value in purchasing "Christian stuff" than they did in giving toward the preaching of the gospel.

KNOW YOUR PLACE OF PROVISION

I (Craig) was teaching this concept of "Sparrow Faith" in one meeting, and a man posed the following question, "Are you saying then that if I believe that God is my source, He will just automatically by His grace make provision for me? If this is so, then I can just quit my job and expect God to provide for me, right?" He was obviously being facetious to make a point. We would all recognize that there is something wrong with this thinking, but what is it? The Lord led me to answer this man's question through a look at the life of Elijah in I Kings chapter 17. I discovered that it is important to recognize the place and channel through which God is making provision. In the case of the man who asked the question, God's channel of provision for him was through his present employment. I believe that many Christians have been confused, because they have missed God's place and channel of provision. Let's look at this account of Elijah's life.

1 KINGS 17

2   *Then the word of the Lord came to him, saying,*

3   *'Get away from here and turn eastward, and hide by the Brook Cherith, which flows into the Jordan.*

4   *And it will be that you shall drink from the brook, and I have commanded the ravens to feed you there.'*

5   *So he went and did according to the word of the Lord, for he went and stayed by the Brook Cherith, which flows into the Jordan.*

6   *The ravens brought him bread and meat in the morning and bread and meat in the evening; and he drank from the brook. (NKJV)*

The first point we see in the life of Elijah is that the word of the Lord came to him. Elijah received specific instruction from the Lord about his place of provision. He was not an atheist looking to money to be a source for him. He was listening to the spirit of God. This same principle is true for us. We need to be in dynamic relationship with the living God in order to know where is our place of provision. Many times in the life of most Christians, God will change the place and channel of provision. It is critical at these times to be listening to the spirit of God so as to know that the channel or place of provision has changed. So Elijah heard from God that although there was a drought and famine in the land, he was to go to the Brook Cherith and ravens would there provide for him bread and meat.

I have noticed that in the lives of many Christians there is a tendency for great fear to come upon them at the times of provision channel changes. I believe that it is important for us to know that the channel and place of provision will change for most of us many times in our lives, but the source of provision remains the same.

Elijah acted on the word he had received from the Lord and moved from where he was to the Brook Cherith. God had not promised him money, only provision. Elijah could have remained where he was, experienced lack of provision, and become angry and bitter at God as a result of the lack. I believe that this happens to many Christians. They simply fail to recognize location and channel changes made by God in their provision. As a result, they find themselves in some place other than the place designated by God for their current provision.

Usually, in order to recognize provision channel changes, it is necessary to have some prior relationship and experience with the Lord. It took some faith in God for Elijah to move from where he was to the brook. I'm sure it took faith to believe that ravens would really bring him food daily. It must have taken faith to eat the meat and bread that the ravens brought. Have you ever thought about where ravens get bread and meat? Let's look a little farther in the story.

1 KINGS 17

7 *And it happened after a while that the brook dried up, because there had been no rain in the land.*

8 *Then the word of the Lord come to him, saying,*

9 *'Arise, go to Zerepath, which belongs to Sidon, and dwell there. See, I have commanded a widow there to provide for you.' (NKJV)*

When the water in the brook dried up, by this time Elijah had probably already learned that termination of provision through a particular channel is pretty indicative of a channel change being made by God. Sure enough, the word of the Lord very quickly followed the drying up of the brook. Most Christians are thrown into a panic every time a particular channel that God has been using for provision dries up. Most people are at these times gripped by the spirit of Mammon, become instant atheists and begin frantically striving in their own strength to solve their provision problem. Sparrow Faith, on the other hand, doesn't abandon the source of provision, but simply recognizes a channel change.

If the man who asked me this question would have simply quit his job and expected God to provide for him in the name of "Sparrow Faith," he would have found himself out of God's place of current provision for his life. It is critical to recognize the location and channel of your provision from God.

I have always thought that another strange part of the instruction that Elijah received from the Lord was that he was to find a widow in Zerepath, and that she would be his next channel of provision. If I had been Elijah, I would have thought that the Lord would send me to a rich person in Zerepath, not to a widow who didn't even have enough provision for herself, let alone for a guest. As I meditated on this passage, I began to see that the Lord had a double purpose in this instruction. He was going to accomplish something in the life of the widow as well as make provision for Elijah. Let's read further.

1 KINGS 17

10 *So he arose and went to Zerepath. And when he came to the gate of the city, indeed a widow was there, gathering sticks. And he called to her and said,' "Please bring me a little water in a cup, that I may drink."*

11 *And as she was going to get it, he called to her and said, "Please, bring me a morsel of bread in your hand."*

12 *So she said, "As the Lord your God lives, I do not have bread, only a handful of flour in a bin, and a little oil in a jar; and see, I am gathering a couple of sticks, that I may go in and prepare it for myself and my son, that we may eat it, and die."*

13 *And Elijah said to her, "Do not fear; go and do as you have said, but make me a small cake from it first, and bring it to me; and afterward make some for yourself and your son."*

14 *For thus says the Lord God of Israel; "The bin of flour shall not be used up, nor shall the jar of oil run dry, until the day the Lord sends rain on the earth."*

15 So she went away and did according to the word of Elijah; and she and he and her household ate for many days.

16 The bin of flour was not used up nor did the jar of oil run dry, according to the word of the Lord which He spoke by Elijah. (NKJV)

Again, this must have taken faith for Elijah to obey the word of the Lord. Can you imagine what it must have been like for Elijah to have to ask a destitute widow to prepare food and drink for him. This would firstly be extremely humbling. Secondly, it would offend your own natural mind. If I had been Elijah, I would have been thinking, "Lord, I must have missed your instruction. This widow is destitute. I shouldn't be asking her to provide for me. I should be taking an offering amongst the rest of the town for her, so that she can live. She says that she is so poor that she is preparing her last meal for her son and herself. Lord, there must be some mistake. I can't ask her to give to me." Wouldn't that just make you feel terrible to have to do what God asked Elijah to do?

Can you imagine meeting a destitute widow who is preparing her last bit of food before she dies, and the Lord tells you to tell her, "Before you prepare that meal, first get me a drink of water and prepare me a small cake and bring it to me."

Why did the Lord have Elijah ask this woman to give him her last little bit of food? I believe that again the issue in this woman's life was Sparrow Faith. In what was she trusting for provision? I believe it is evident that she was trusting in her supply of flour and oil. Since these had run out, she was now expecting to die. God wanted to move her faith from the material provision to the living God. He wanted to be her source of provision. How did he choose to accomplish this? He had the man of God ask her to give him her last bit of material provision. This removed her ability to trust in the flour and oil for sustenance.

God was not after her flour and oil, nor was Elijah. God was after her faith. He wanted to be her source. I believe that many times this same thing is true regarding men of God receiving offerings today. Some people feel that they are after the money. Not all have right motives, but I believe that most of the time the man of God is not after people's money. He and God are after their faith. Faith in God releases miracles.

When the widow did what Elijah asked her to do, she released a supernatural miracle of God. The oil and flour did not run out for many days. She learned to live by trusting the word of the Lord instead of material possessions.

I (Craig) remember the first time I was asked by the Lord to do something similar to what Elijah had to do in this account. Several years ago, I worked full time in a Christian counseling ministry. This ministry was supported by the donations of those who came for ministry. As counselors, we asked each person to whom we ministered to pray at the end of each session and ask the Lord what they were to give as an offering that day.

After ministering to one young man, I asked him to pray about what to give as an offering that day. He responded that we didn't even need to pray, as he was destitute, and had absolutely nothing to give. In my natural mind, I wanted to give to him. However, I felt the spirit of God rise up in me and I found myself saying to him, "I don't believe you. Show me your wallet." He opened his wallet, and sure enough he had nothing.

I then said to him "I know you have something to give. Empty your pockets." He did, and out came fifty cents. "I knew you had something!" I said. I watched terror strike his face as he said, "That fifty cents is all I have, and I need all of it to get home on the bus. I got this fifty cents by returning soda pop bottles to the grocery store. It's snowing outside. I live sixteen miles away from here and it costs fifty cents to get home on the bus. I need the whole fifty cents for bus fare."

My heart went out to this man, but I also realized that his trust was in his fifty cents, not in God. Mammon had him bound in fear and love of money. Neither God nor I was after his money. We were both after his faith. He was a practical atheist. God was not in his thinking of how he would get home. So, I told him, "Since the bus costs fifty cents, if you give, then you place yourself in the position of being a candidate for a miracle. We're going to pray to ask the Lord how much of the fifty cents you are to give in the offering this afternoon. You have to know that I am not interested in your money. You could give the entire fifty cents and it wouldn't really make a great deal of difference to this ministry."

I felt a little badly for this fellow as I had to speak quite sternly to him. It seemed a bit strange to take the last fifty cents from an indigent man who had nothing. However, I knew that if I didn't press this point with him, he would never be free of the spirit of Mammon, who had kept him in poverty through his trust in money for a long time. He finally agreed, and we prayed. He felt that he was to give five cents. I had to make change for him. We then prayed over his five-cent offering. He renounced his trust in money, declared his independence from the spirit of Mammon, and his reliance upon the Lord Jesus Christ as his source of provision.

This man then went out of my office, still grumbling about how he was now going to have to walk home sixteen miles in the snow, because he didn't have enough money for the bus fare. Next week when he returned, this man had, as you might suspect, a great miracle story. He told me that when he arrived at the bus stop, still angry, he looked down and there at the base of the bus stop sign was a nickel. He picked it up and thought to himself, "Boy, that sure was lucky." He said it didn't even dawn on him until he was halfway home that the nickel he "happened" to find was the provision of the Lord for his ride home. When he got home, he then found an unexpected check in the mail for five dollars. He considered this a one hundred-fold return on his offering of five cents. When the man came for his appointment the next week, he was so excited about the offering, he could hardly wait for the counseling session to be over, so he could give in the offering and exercise his faith in God as his source again. I can't remember exactly, but he had something like a total of two dollars to pray about that second week. This man grew in faith and finances week by week. The five-cent offering I received from him turned out to be the key that broke his trust in money and began to prove to him God's faithfulness as a source of provision.

JUDGMENT AND DELIVERANCE

For many people I (Earl) have found it is not enough to simply pray a perfunctory prayer and declare, "I don't love money." There is also a need for judgment and deliverance. This comes through putting action to faith, demonstration of trust in God as source. Jesus demonstrated this in His encounter with the rich young ruler.

MARK 10

17 *Now as He was going out on his journey, a man ran up and knelt before Him, 'Teacher, (You are essentially and perfectly morally) good, what must I do to inherit eternal life (that is, to partake of eternal salvation in the Messiah's kingdom)?'*

18 *And Jesus said to him, 'Why do you call me good? There is no one good except God alone.*

19 *You know the commandments: do not kill; do not commit adultery; do not steal; do not bear false witness; do not defraud; honor your father and your mother.'*

20 *And he replied to Him, 'Teacher, I have carefully guarded and observed all these and taken care not to violate them from my boyhood.'*

21 *And Jesus looking upon him loved him, and He said to him, 'You lack one thing; go and sell all you have and give the (money) to the poor, and you will have Treasure In Heaven; and come (and) accompany Me— walking the same road that I walk.'*

22 *At that saying the man's countenance fell and was gloomy, and he went away grieved and sorrowing, for he was holding great possessions. (Amplified)*

In order for us to understand this story, we need an explanation of a particular Jewish idiom. When a person called someone "good," he was positioning himself with the understanding that he will be obedient to whatever that person counsels him to do. Jesus tests the young man by saying that there is no one good but God and proceeds to quote six of the ten commandments. Notice that the rich young ruler responds by stating that he has kept those commandments since he was a boy. He understood what it means to call someone "good." Now Jesus is ready to counsel him. Verse 21 tells us that Jesus looked at him and loved him. He did not despise this man, but rather He loved him. Jesus realized that this man was in bondage to the spirit of Mammon. In His compassion, Jesus quotes only six of the Ten Commandments to which the young ruler could reply in the affirmative. There was a conflict of love between God and Mammon. Jesus prescribed an act of spiritual warfare, to move into Mammon's territory, by converting all he had into money and then GIVING it away. He wanted him delivered from the grip of the spirit of Mammon. Jesus was not after the man's money, He was after the allegiance of his heart. The man went away sorrowing and grieving for he was holding great possessions. Riches had a grip on him! He was blinded to the love of Jesus and blind to the scriptures.

Proverbs 19:17 states that he who gives to the poor lends to the Lord and the Lord will repay. I would have to ask this man, "What is the problem? Jesus asked you to give only to the poor. You are simply lending to the Lord and He will repay you." However, when the Mammon spirit has a hold on your mind, you see only loss and great lack. Jesus wanted him to profane Mammon, thereby breaking its desire, the bondage in his life. He was unable to do so even though he had called Jesus good!

It is interesting to note in the ensuing conversation with the disciples, that in verse 24, "the disciples were amazed and bewildered and perplexed at His words." Why were they this way? I believe it is because many of them were quite wealthy and probably had money in their pockets also. In verse 26 it says that they were "shocked and exceedingly astonished," and said to Him and to one another, "Then who can be saved?" I am sure their question was "Jesus, if that's what he had to do to enter the Kingdom of God, what about us? We have money!. Do we have to do the same?" When Jesus called Simon (Peter), James and John, sons of Zebedee, who were partners in business with Simon, the Word says that after they had run their boats on shore, they left everything and followed Jesus

(Luke 5:10,11). They were businessmen and left it all. The Mammon spirit had no hold on their lives.

Another example is found in Matthew 9:9 in which Jesus saw Matthew sitting at the tax collector's office. He called Matthew to be His disciple, and immediately Matthew rose and followed Him. One would think that if there were going to be a Mammon influence in a person's life, it would be in the life of a tax collector! Matthew straightway followed Jesus. It is no wonder that the disciples were bewildered and shocked at what Jesus said to the rich young ruler. However, the same requirement did not apply to the disciples, as they were not under the domination of the Mammon spirit.

Of course, there was one disciple, Judas, who was controlled by Mammon, and when he saw Mary pouring ointment on Jesus' feet, he said:

JOHN 12

5   *"Why was this perfume not sold for three hundred denarii, (a year's wages for an ordinary workman) and that (money) given to the poor (the destitute)?"*

6   *Now he did not say this because he cared for the poor, but because he was a thief; and having the bag (the money box, the purse of the twelve), he took for himself what was put into it (pilfering the collections). (Amplified)*

Where had Judas heard those words, which now came out of his mouth? He was there when Jesus spoke to the rich young ruler. He was attempting to appear very spiritual. I (Earl) have had people ask me, "Does everybody need to do what Jesus told the rich young ruler to do?" I have answered, "I don't know. You will have to ask the Lord. But it could be that if you had to ask that question, then you probably do!" The issue is, "In what do you trust? Who is the source, God or Mammon? Do you love and pursue God or money?"

In reality, everything we have we receive as a gift from God. Our usage of money is simply a test to see if we understand God's grace. Do I see my provision as a gift from Him, or as something I am owed as a result of my works? Do I use money in giving and receiving to introduce others to grace, or only in the world system of buying and selling to obtain something of equal value? When we give that which was created by man for buying and selling (money) with no expectation of return, we introduce others to grace and profane the sacred properties that Mammon would attempt to ascribe to money. Giving is an act of spiritual warfare in which we proclaim that money has no power in our lives. My ability to accomplish my goals is in no way diminished by decreasing the current amount of money over which I have stewardship. Since God is able to have money released to me out of the world system, my capacity is in no way diminished through giving. God is my source and my trust is in His provision for me by His grace.

CHAPTER 3
TWO REALMS:
TWO DIFFERENT ECONOMIC
SYSTEMS

KINGDOM OF GOD	REALM OF SATAN "WORLD SYSTEM"
Operative Economic Principle GIVING & RECEIVING	Operative Economic Principle BUYING & SELLING

Most Christians would recognize that there exist side by side on the earth two separate and independent realms: the Kingdom of God and the realm of Satan. There are also two totally separate and independent economic systems operative within these two domains. The world system operates under the power of Satan, (I John 5:19). The spirit of Mammon works through buying and selling and governs the monetary system. This is in contrast to the Kingdom of God, which is governed by Jesus Christ and operates on the principles of giving and receiving. Increase in the world system comes through addition and percentage increase. Increase in God's economy comes through multiplication, 30-, 60- and 100-fold or an optimum yield, which may be greater than or disproportionate to what was sown (Matthew 25:14-30; Luke 19:11-27).

Many people are unfamiliar with the multiplication of the Kingdom of God. All they have known all their lives is percentage increase and addition. Most people feel that if they could get a 20% or 30% annual return on their money that this would be a very good investment. Within the context of the world system it may be, but in contrast to the 300%, 600% or 1,000% increase or a maximum yield available in God's system of finances, this would be a very poor investment.

DISTINCTION BETWEEN WEALTH, RICHES & MONEY

Most people have thought that wealth, riches and money were interchangeable terms for the same thing. We believe that these terms need to be carefully defined, as they are descriptive of different things and are governed differently. Wealth is created by and governed by God. Money is created by man, and is influenced by the spirit of Mammon. Riches are in between wealth and money and can come under the influence of Mammon so that we trust and serve them.

The mention of wealth and riches is noted in Solomon's request to God.

2 CHRONICLES 1

10 *"Give me now wisdom and knowledge to go out and come in before this people for who can rule this your people that is so great?"*

11 *God replied to Solomon, "Because this was in your heart, and you have not asked for riches, possessions (wealth), honor and glory, or the life of your foes or even long life, but had asked for wisdom and knowledge for yourself that you may rule and judge my people over whom I have made you king,*

12 *wisdom and knowledge are granted you and I will give you riches, possessions (wealth), honor and glory, such as none of the kings had before you, and none after you shall have their equal." (Amplified)*

Wealth in the Hebrew language is defined as a resource, substance, goods, strength and a force, and possessions. Riches can also be used to serve the purposes of God and His Kingdom.

Firstly, what is wealth? We believe that wealth is that which has inherent, intrinsic value, and was created by God. When we look in the Old Testament, we find examples of wealthy people. God had blessed them and they were co-owners with God. The wealth they had was land, houses, cattle and flocks, gold, silver, in the form of bullion or jewelry, timber, oil, gas, natural resources, and people in the form of Maid and Men servants. We see an example of this in the life of Abram.

GENESIS 13

2   *A bram was very rich in livestock, in silver and in gold.*
    (NKJV)

These commodities all have intrinsic value. An ounce of gold today would buy about the same amount of food that it would have fifty years ago, even though the value in money of one ounce of gold is vastly different today. Thus, when the Lord stated in Deuteronomy 8:18, "It is He who gives you the power (or ability) to get (or make) wealth," this does not refer to money, but rather to wealth. Many Christians, on the basis of this scripture, are caught up in the pursuit of money.

One of God's purposes for wealth was that it might be an inheritance. Wealth was to increase from generation to generation. God revealed himself as the God of Abraham, Isaac and Jacob, a God of three successive generations.

PROVERBS 13

22   *A good man leaves an inheritance to his children's children*
     and the wealth of the sinner [finds its way eventually] in to
     the hands of the righteous, for whom it was laid up.
     (A mplified)

Note the wealth transfer of the inheritance is for your grand-children! When you and I pass on, they are the ones who are to benefit at their young age, so they can go and fulfill God's plan and purpose in their lives.

PROVERBS 10

15   The rich man's wealth is his strong city; the poverty of the poor is their ruin. (Amplified)

Returning again to Jesus' encounter with the rich young ruler, we find His disciples questioning Him about His statement regarding the rich entering the Kingdom. In his answer to His disciples, Jesus concludes with the following statement:

MARK 10

29   "Assuredly, I say to you, there is no one who has left houses or brothers or sister or father or mother or wife or children or lands, for My sake and the gospel's,

30   who shall not receive a hundredfold now in this time—houses and brothers and sisters and mothers and children and lands, with persecutions—and in the age to come eternal life." (NKJV)

It is interesting to note that Jesus did not mention money in this verse. Jesus did not say to give up all your money and you will receive a hundred-fold return. Rather, the Word of God treats money differently from the wealth of land, houses, and people relationships. Jesus did not promise a multiplied return of money to anyone, but rather, that those who had given up wealth would receive a multiplied return of wealth

What then is money? Money is simply a receptacle of deferred goods and services created by man for trading. It is a medium of exchange for which one may trade goods or services. It has been described as the harvest of our production. Money is what we receive for our production and service as persons, which we can then use to obtain the production and services of others. Money has no intrinsic value, but its value is determined on a daily basis by markets. A market, in actuality, is nothing more than the opinions of people. In other words, money is worth whatever people say it is worth. Money also carries no intrinsic morality, but rather is an amoral commodity that is neither virtuous nor evil. Money traditionally has been fashioned out of metal, paper, or plastic into coins or notes, imprinted with the image of some important man or woman.

Money is classically defined by these five generic characteristics.

1. Money is divisible. It must be fashioned in divisible units for trading.

2. Money is durable. It must not readily disintegrate and thus lose its tradability. Even paper money has lasting qualities beyond notebook paper.

3. Money is transportable. It must not be so heavy or cumbersome that it cannot be readily transported by its holder for daily trading.

4. Money is easily recognizable. It must be evident to all that it is a readily accepted medium of exchange.

5. Money is scarce. There must be a significantly smaller supply of it than there is demand. The quantity in circulation must be able to be controlled. If not properly managed, mismanagement causes inflation or deflation.

When asked the question, to whom does money belong? Most Christians would respond that it all belongs to God. However, when questioned by Pharisees on the issue of taxes, Jesus very clearly taught that money is not created by God and does not belong to God. Money, instead, is created by man and belongs to the world system.

MATTHEW 22

17 *"'Tell us therefore, what do You think? Is it lawful to pay taxes to Caesar, or not?"*

18 *But Jesus perceived their wickedness, and said, "Why do you test Me, you hypocrites?*

19 *Show Me the tax money." So they brought Him a denarius.*

20 *And He said to them, "Whose image and inscription is this?"*

21 They said to Him, "Caesar's." And He said to them, "Render therefore to Caesar the things that are Caesar's and to God the things that are God's." (NKJV)

Although Jesus in this passage was answering a question about taxes, He was also very clearly teaching about the nature of money. The denarius coin did not belong to God, but rather to Caesar. When one takes a chunk of gold, which has inherent value, and is by nature wealth, molds it, prints an image of man's face on it, and dedicates it to be used for buying and selling, this chunk of gold has changed kingdoms. It no longer has God's ownership, but now belongs to the world system. It is now not a part of God's system, but rather a part of Caesar's economic system. God has released it into that system.

Some people have tried to use money as a store or value or wealth. Storing wealth by accumulating money typically has lower transaction costs than storing wealth in the form of houses, land, bullion etc. These forms must be sold when the wealth is harvested for consumption. Money is subject to the weaknesses of the Mammon system such as inflation or deflation. Man has tried to offset this weakness by backing all money in circulation with gold (wealth). There is a case to be made for this action when one follows the increase in inflation in countries after they rescind the gold standard. Thus, while wealth belongs to God, money does not. Money is not created by God, but rather by man, and it belongs to the world system. **How then are we as believers to relate to money?** The Word of God refers to money as a little thing or something little. In Matt 25, Jesus tells a parable about three servants who were given talents (a unit of money at that time, which some scholars believe was equal to 75 pounds of gold coinage) to manage on behalf of a master. In verse 27 Jesus rebukes the faithless servant who buried in the ground the money he was given to manage. Jesus told him that he should have at least invested the money in the bank and returned the money with interest. In verses 21 and 23 Jesus commends the first two servants saying, *"Well done, good and faithful servant! You have been faithful over little; I will make you ruler over much. Enter into the joy of your master."* The "little" to which Jesus is specifically referring in this passage is money.

LUKE 16

*10 He who is faithful in a very little [thing], is faithful also in
much; and he who is dishonest and unjust in a very little
[thing] is dishonest and unjust also in much. (Amplified)*

Jesus uses this same word "little" again in reference to money,
the subject of this parable. God uses money to teach faithfulness and
stewardship. Then in verse 12, He is still talking about money,

LUKE 16

*12 And if you have not proven faithful in that which belongs to
another, who will give you that which is your own? (NKJV)*

Jesus is talking to His disciples and states that money belongs to
another, namely to Caesar, or the world system. Thus, we are not to
be governed by money, but rather to govern money. Money is meant
to be our slave, which we direct in service to benefit the Kingdom of
God. We are to be stewards of that which belongs to the world
system, not violators of the basic principles that govern its operation
in that system. We, as Christians, live in the world system, but we are
not of that system. It is not wrong to buy and sell. However, we have
Kingdom principles that overcome the limitations of the world
system.

Another way that we know money does not belong to God is
that we are to love that which God has created and owns. God has
created people, and we are commanded to love one another. If He
had created money and were its owner, then we could love money.
However, we are specifically instructed NOT to love money, for the
love of money is the root of all evil (I Tim. 6:10). **The Hebrew root
word for silver is** *kehsef* [3], **which has come to mean money.**

---

[3] James Strong, *Strong's Exhaustive Concordance of the Bible*, Baker
Book House, Grand Rapids, Michigan 1985, n.d. *kehsef* (# H 3701)

Kehsef comes from the root word that means to desire or languish after.

When wealth is converted into money, it changes kingdoms, and people managing it become subject to the spirit of Mammon in a way they weren't before. Time after time, I (Craig) have encountered people who have sold property such as a family farm, divided the money between the children or grandchildren, only to find that none of them has any of the money left within a few short years. What happened? While the farm remained in the form of wealth, no one perceived it as having purchasing power. Its value was simply the realistic value of the farm. However, the moment the farm was sold, the wealth was converted into money and thereby changed kingdoms. Mammon then was able to create in the minds of the heirs an inordinate ascribing of power and value to the money. People many times have no idea how powerful the spirit of Mammon is in ascribing sacred properties to money. Another very potent example of the power Mammon has over the minds of people regarding money is recorded in the book of Acts.

ACTS 4-5

34 *Nor was there a destitute or needy person among them, for as many as were owners of land or houses proceeded to sell them, and one by one they brought (gave back) the amount received from the sales*

35 *And laid it at the feet of the apostles. Then distribution was made according as any one had need.*

36 *Now Joseph, a Levite and native of Cyprus who was surnamed Barnabas by the apostles which means, Son of Encouragement,*

37 *Sold a field which belonged to him, and brought the sum of money and laid it at the feet of the apostles.*

1 *But a certain man named Ananias, with his wife Sapphira sold a piece of property.*

2 *And with his wife's knowledge and connivance he kept back and wrongfully appropriated some of the*

> *proceedings, bringing a part only and putting it at the feet of the apostles.*
>
> 3 *But Peter said, "Ananias, why has Satan filled your heart that you should (in violation of your promise) withdraw secretly and appropriate to your own use part of the price from the sale of the land?*
>
> 4 *As long as it remained unsold, was it not still your own? And (even) after it was sold, was not (the money) at your disposal and under your control? Why then, is it that you have proposed and purposed in your heart to do this thing?— How could you have the heart to do such a deed? You have not (simply) lied to men— playing false and showing yourself utterly deceitful— but to God."*
>
> 5 *Upon hearing these words, Ananias fell down and died. And great dread and terror took possession of all who heard of it. (Amplified)*

The example had been set in the early church where people had converted wealth to money and given it to meet needs of people. I am sure that Ananias and Sapphira saw these examples and thought it was a good idea, perhaps even as something they could do so people would think well of them.

Ananias and Sapphira had no idea the type of pressure that would come against them by the spirit of Mammon the moment they converted their wealth into money. Obviously, they would have been far better off to have given the deed to the land to the apostles rather than the money. While their offering was in the form of wealth, they were happy to give the entire amount of land to the apostles. However, the moment it was converted into money, their thinking changed. They were impacted by Mammon to ascribe power to money, and then it entered into their minds to withhold some of the money from the apostles, thereby reneging on their commitment to God. This powerfully demonstrates the impact of the spirit of Mammon on a person's mind.

I would guess that Ananias and Sapphira probably received a greater sum of money for their land than they had expected. They then began to think that maybe they would give to the apostles only the amount of money, which they had originally thought the land was worth. Since no on else really knew how much they had received, no one would be the wiser. Isn't it amazing how quickly God is removed from the thinking when the spirit of Mammon grips one's mind? What atheistic thinking! "No one will know," they thought. What about the Holy Spirit?

The end result in this event was that Ananias and Sapphira lost their lives due to eliminating God from their financial system. This account demonstrates to us the power of the spirit of Mammon to deceive, then subsequently steal, destroy and ultimately kill (the very nature of the enemy). We see this truth experientially manifested in the way wealth is often released to Christian ministries and churches. Properties, buildings, commodities come easily into the hands of these organizations, many times simply as a blessing from God. However, when it comes to money for Christian endeavor, it is usually a story of never enough. Money has to be extracted out of the world system and pressed into service for Kingdom use. Because money belongs to the world system rather than to God, even Christians must adhere to the rules governing the management of money in the world system. In order for money to be released to Christians to press into service for Kingdom use, the spirit of Mammon must be dealt with and the rules governing money must be obeyed. Many Christians regularly violate the rules governing the world system of money and then expect God to supernaturally provide money for their Kingdom endeavors. This is similar to violating the law of gravity and expecting God to overrule it because we are serving Him. No, even ministers and missionaries must comply with gravity.

The devil governs the world system (1 John 5:19), and he knows the rules by which it operates. Satan is a legalist and works our lack of knowledge of the laws governing money and its usage against us. If God simply overruled on our behalf the natural laws of the world system, then Satan would have a valid accusation against God regarding justice. However when we have complied with the rules of the world system, we can apply Kingdom principles of finance in faith and have the confident expectation that there will be financial release. We can be absolutely confident when our faith in God does not waiver on the spirit side, and we have met the conditions of the natural laws of the world system regarding money on the truth side. Then we can ask God in faith for finances without wavering, hesitating, or doubting (James 1:6).

Peter, as a staff member of Jesus' ministry, was once questioned as to whether Jesus would cooperate with the secular tax collectors.

MATTHEW 17

24 *When they arrived in Capernaum, the collectors of the half-shekel [the temple tax] went up to Peter and said, "Does not your Teacher pay the half-shekel?"*

25 *He answered, "Yes." And when he came home, Jesus spoke to him [about it] first, saying, "What do you think, Simon? From whom do earthly rulers collect duties or tribute? From their own sons or from others not of their own family?"*

26 *And when Peter said, 'From other people— not of their own family'— Jesus said to him, 'Then the sons are exempt.*

27 *However, in order not to give offense and cause them to stumble— that is to judge unfavorably and unjustly— go down to the sea and throw in a hook; take the first fish that comes up, and when you open its mouth you will find there a shekel. Take it and give it to them to pay the temple tax for Me and for yourself.' (Amplified)*

The finances of Jesus' ministry were operated in accord with the bureaucracy of secular taxation. Jesus told Peter that although they were not really part of the world's monetary system, they should still act in accord with that system in order not to give an offense either to believers or unbelievers. Spiritually, they were exempt from taxation; they submitted themselves to avoid any hindrance to preaching of the gospel. Jesus had faith that God would supply their necessities, regardless of the financial demands.

A book by Charles Blair, entitled, "A Man Who Could Do No Wrong,"[4] illustrates this point. Charles had a vision from God to create a building for the living and care of senior citizens. The vision was no doubt a wonderful plan from God. However, the way he raised money for the project violated the U.S. Securities and Exchange Commission rules. Since this pastor may have believed that money belonged to God, thus he could raise money for a given project and use it for another God idea. A violation of rules in the world system took place, which states that funds raised for a specific project must be used for that project! It was a sad story and a rich learning experience for Charles in the handling of money which is governed by and accountable to the world system. In the end, Charles was indicted on several counts of SEC law violations. He became a living testimony to the fact that one cannot violate the system to which money belongs and then expect God to override such mismanagement. **What about the third category of finances we mentioned, riches?** Are riches also to be distinguished from wealth and money? We believe so. We would define riches as money working for you. When you have money in excess of your obligations and necessities, you are in a position to invest this money and have it work for you. Thus, riches are not based on money that you worked for, but rather on money that works for you. Once you have money working for you, by definition you have riches. Today, riches are most commonly found in the form of stocks, bonds, mutual funds, government securities etc.

When we place money in this category, **the Mammon spirit will try to influence us to trust in these investments**, especially for our future needs. Paul in his writing to Timothy tells him to charge the rich men not to be proud and trust in riches, but rather in God.

---

[4] Charles Blair, *A Man Who Could Do No Wrong*, Chosen Books Publishing Co Ltd., Lincoln, Virginia, 1981

1 TIMOTHY 6

17 As for the rich in this world, charge them not to be proud and arrogant and contemptuous of others, nor to set their hopes on uncertain riches, but on God, Who richly and ceaselessly provides us with everything for [our] enjoyment; (Amplified)

Again Paul is here declaring that God, rather than riches, is our source.

Jesus talks about the fact that riches are deceitful. In Mark, chapter 4, the sower sows the Word in several different types of soil, but various hindrances are identified which destroy the fruitfulness of the Word. One of the prime hindrances that Jesus mentions is weeds, described as deceitful riches, which choke out the ability of the Word to grow and thrive (verse 19).

Having money that works for us is not wrong. In fact, the parables of the talents (Matthew 25) and the minas (Luke 19) is about taking money that has been given to us and making it work for us to provide multiplication. In other words, to have it create riches. We must be honest with God as to its purpose. Some people save for a rainy day, rather than for something specific, such as a child's education or replacement of a car. Riches that are not identified for a specific purpose can be used by Mammon to influence our hearts and minds to trust in them. When the stock market takes a plunge, people who trust in riches have jumped out of building windows to their death. Their trust was in those riches that had just lost significant value. Riches can be used in the creation of wealth or as a storage receptacle for money. Jesus commended those servants who multiplied the money given to them by having it work for them;, however it was returned to the master. God wants overflow of money in our life, for us to have it working and ready when the Master calls for it. When we ask God for the purpose of the overflow, He may instruct us to turn it into riches so it will work for us for now, or He has purposes for it in the future. I (Earl) call this, "the Master has need of" funds. Money or riches that are available for Kingdom use, as soon as the Lord calls for them!

We have seen now that God takes ownership of wealth. He desires wealth in your hands in joint ownership to be a blessing generationally. Now, if we convert wealth into money, we introduce the spirit of Mammon immediately. The story of the prodigal son is a case in point.

LUKE 15

11   *And He (Jesus) said, There was a certain man who had two sons;*

12   *And the younger of them said to his father, Father, give me the part of the property that falls [to me]. And he divided the livelihood [between] them.*

13   *And not many days after that the younger son gathered up all that he had and journeyed into a distant country, and there he wasted his fortune in reckless and loose-from-restraint living, (Amplified)*

Note that the younger son received his inheritance of property and converted it into money and wasted it in reckless living. The Mammon influence is now present once the inheritance is in the form of money.

Many countries have laws that prohibit minors from receiving inheritances of wealth until the age of 21, to prevent it from being converted into money and squandered. The laws attempt to deal with Mammon without specifically understanding the spirit realm. However, everyone sees its effects in the lives of young people.

SPIRITUAL WARFARE OVER FINANCES

We have already established that money has been created by the world system in order to carry on buying and selling. Jesus told us to pay to Caesar the things that are due to Caesar and pay to God the things that are due to God (Matthew 22:2). We are all created in God's image, and thus belong to Him. As Christians, we are simply stewards of that which belongs to another. Money belongs to the world's system. However, we are stewards of that which is released to us through the exchange of our creativity and time. God teaches us faithfulness and stewardship through our handling of money.

Now, it is the Lord's purpose to release much money into our hands out of the world's system for use in the Kingdom of God over our lifetime. With money in our hands, we can force the world system to do work for the Kingdom of God. We can then buy airplane tickets and evangelize in any place in the world. We can print Bibles and distribute them. With money we can give the cup of cold water in Jesus' name to many persons in the world all at the same time. We can physically only be at one place at a time, but money given to ministries around the world give us the opportunity of a form of omnipresence! Because a Christian has this potential, the devil will do all in his power to keep money out of the hands of Christians when he finds that one who is not controlled by the Mammon spirit and is committed to spreading the Gospel. On the other hand, the devil may place vast amounts of money into a person's hands, when that person can be controlled by the spirit of Mammon. If the person is not disciplined in the handling of finances, such abundance may destroy him/her by diverting focus away from the Kingdom to the pursuit of more riches. However, Jesus has given us authority in His Name over all the works of the enemy. Therefore, we can wage spiritual warfare against the enemy for release of money and maintaining proper focus on the work of the Kingdom of God. This battle is spoken of in the scripture cited below.

1 TIMOTHY 6

9   *But those who crave to be rich fall into temptation and a snare, and into many foolish (useless, godless) and hurtful desires that plunge men into ruin and destruction and miserable perishing.*

10   *For the love of money is a root of all evils; it is through this craving that some have been led astray, and have wandered from the faith and pierced themselves through with many acute [mental] pangs.*

11   *Flee from all these things; aim at and pursue righteousness— that is, right standing with God and true goodness; godliness*

(which is the loving fear of God and Christ likeness), faith, love, steadfastness (patience) and gentleheartedness.

12   <u>*Fight the good fight of the faith;*</u> *lay hold of the eternal life to which you were summoned, and confessed the good confession [of faith] before many witnesses. (Amplified)*

It is interesting to note that verse 12 is in a money section of this chapter. We are to wage spiritual warfare in the fight of faith over the release of money. Spiritual warfare is more than commanding in the Name of Jesus that certain activities be initiated or terminated. Spiritual warfare is waged by how we choose to live and function. When the devil was coming to Jesus in John 14, notice Jesus' response.

JOHN 14

30   *'I will not talk with you much more, for the prince (evil genius, ruler) of the world is coming. And he has no claim on Me— he has nothing in common with Me, there is nothing in Me that belongs to him, he has no power over Me.' (Amplified)*

We cannot be walking in violation of principles in the world system (mishandling debt, or misappropriating finances, for example) that govern finances and expect to have authority in the spirit realm over the spirit of Mammon. Committing to bring our personal finances in order and taking definite steps to do that through repentance, releases authority in our words and life to wage spiritual warfare successfully. May there be nothing in our handling of finances that gives the enemy a right to withhold or stop the flow of finances into our hands!

Now faith comes by hearing and hearing by the Word of God (Romans 10:17). **We have found that faith involves at least the following three things:**

1.   We must believe what the Word of God says.

2.   We must confess the Word. In other words, our own ears need to hear what it is that we believe.

3. Our actions must line up with our believing and confessing. Now how does this apply to the area of finances?

We must be firmly grounded in the Word of God concerning finances. The battle over the release of finances in our lives must be won in the spirit realm first before it can be manifested in the physical realm. We need to grasp the understanding of how the Kingdom of God functions financially. We must further resolve to operate in Kingdom principles and not be swayed by the world's system of financial thinking. Our actions must line up with our belief and confession. We must not be doubleminded as Apostle James discusses.

JAMES 1

5   *If any of you is deficient in wisdom, let him ask of the giving God [Who gives] to every one liberally and ungrudgingly, without reproaching or faultfinding, and it will be given him.*

6   *Only it must be in faith that he asks, with no wavering— no hesitating, no doubting. For the one who wavers (hesitates, doubts) is like the billowing surge out at sea, that is blown hither and thither and tossed by the wind.*

7   *For truly, let not such a person imagine that he will receive anything [he asks for] from Lord.*

8   *[For being as he is] a man of two minds— hesitating, dubious, irresolute and uncertain about everything (he thinks, feels, decides). (Amplified)*

EPHESIANS 6

12 *For we wrestle not against flesh and blood, but against principalities and against powers, against the rulers of the darkness of this world, against spiritual wickedness in high places. (NKJV)*

The spirit of Mammon is wanting to govern the minds and hearts of people as we have seen in the previous chapters. The Mammon spirit is operating as a power in the spirit realm to control the affairs of men in the financial arena.

We are all acquainted with people who formerly were loving God and serving Him. However, when money was released into their hands, such ones were captured by a love for the money, did not use it for the Kingdom of God, and are not loving and serving God today. We have observed that we are presently in a spiritual battle in the financial arena, which is perhaps more intense than at any time in past history. The conflict between the world system and the Kingdom of God for the hearts and minds of men and women regarding finances is huge. However, the weapons of our warfare are not of human design.

2 CORINTHIANS 10

4   *For the weapons of our warfare are not physical (weapons of flesh and blood), but they are mighty before God for the overthrow and destruction of strongholds,*

5   *[Inasmuch as we] refute arguments and theories and reasonings and every proud and lofty thing that sets itself up against the (true) knowledge of God; and we lead every thought and purpose away captive into the obedience of Christ, the Messiah, the Anointed One.*

6   *Being in readiness to punish every [insubordinate for his] disobedience, when your own submission and obedience [as a church] are fully secured and complete. (Amplified)*

As you read the rest of this book, may God give you revelation of your personal battle in this arena. May you also receive His empowerment of your will and desire to stand against the enemy who would try to keep finances from your hands or divert your attention from your service to the Kingdom of God.

PROSPERITY WITH A PURPOSE

As we prepare for the next building block, it is necessary to understand God's plan for prospering His people. Much has been taught about prosperity in the Body of Christ over the years. There has been and still continues to be a reaction to the message, both positive and negative. The positive news is that God's desire is to prosper His people! Thus, we have been blessed with all spiritual blessings or privileges. Everything pertaining to life and godliness has been freely given to us, including wealth, peace, joy and health. You and I have a covenant with Him that is sealed by the blood of Jesus. Living under the covenant is part of the intimate relationship we have with God. If you have faith in your relationship with Him, then you will have faith in the covenant. In the covenant is the promise of provision and prosperity.

Let us first look at the meaning of the word prosperity. The basic word does not refer to money, riches or wealth. It simply means to excel, or to rise to the highest place. It comes from excellent or highness. Thus, to prosper is to go to the highest place in something desirable, whether that desire is spiritual, pertaining to the soul, physical, relational or financial. In this understanding, the key is the word desire. The desire can be for good or evil. If prosperity is to be used for good, then a definition would be as follows: **Biblical prosperity is the ability to use God's power and knowledge to meet the needs of mankind in any realm of life.** God's desire is for His people to have access to His power and knowledge, by the Spirit of God for good to be accomplished.

In the spirit realm, prosperity comes to people when the Gospel is preached and people are born again by receiving Jesus as Savior and Lord. The Gospel is the power of God unto salvation to everyone who believes. Through the new birth people begin to prosper spiritually. One has passed from death to life, the "zoe" or eternal life having recreated the human spirit.

Prosperity in the soul realm affects the mind, will and emotions. Having one's mind continually renewed by the Word of God, brings a change of thinking patterns.

ROMANS 12

2   *Do not be conformed to this world— this age, fashioned after and adapted to its external, superficial customs. But be transformed (changed) by its new ideals and its new attitude— so that you may prove [for yourselves] what is the good and acceptable and perfect will of God, even the thing which is good and acceptable and perfect [in His sight for you]. (Amplified)*

Reading, meditating on, and responding to the Word of God changes our thinking from conformity to the world system to that of Kingdom principles and ways. Such activities transform the mind and prosperity of mind results. A spirit of poverty can affect our thinking. If it is not dealt with, one will always see others as trying to take something away and will be motivated to continually protect self. The resultant attitude will certainly hinder ones giving.

Our will is also meant by God to prosper. It is in reality to be set free from bondages, so we can be obedient to God without delays. Delayed obedience is disobedience.

The Lord also intends for our emotions to prosper. Emotions are to come in line with our choices. Many times very powerful negative feelings will hinder us from making correct choices. Emotions need to be cleansed by the Blood of Jesus Christ, thus empowering our emotions to support right choices, rather than our being tormented with fear, shame, pride, greed and other such compelling feelings. Emotions are meant to under gird our right choices, not to distract us from making them.

ISAIAH 1

19   *If you are willing and obedient, you shall eat the good of the land. (Amplified)*

God desires prosperity of body for us as well. He has provided health and healing for our physical bodies.

3 JOHN

2 *Beloved, I pray that you may prosper in every way and [that
your body] may keep well, even as [I know] your soul keeps
well and prospers. (Amplified)*

Note the sequence— soul prosperity leads to bodily health and
wellness. There are many scriptures both in the Old and New
Testament, that tell us of God's desire for bodily prosperity.

God's desire is for us also to prosper in our relationships with
people: husbands and wives, children and parents, other family
members, the Body of Christ at large, and with everyone.

ROMANS 12

16 *Live in harmony with one another; do not be haughty
(snobbish, high minded, exclusive), but readily adjust
yourself to [people, things] and give yourselves to humble
tasks. Never overestimate yourself or be wise in your own
conceits.*

18 *If possible, as far as it depends on you, live at peace with
every one. (Amplified)*

The secret is living in a humble manner. The Word of God
teaches us how to do this. It is God's desire for us to prosper in our
relationships. Prosperity in the financial realm is also God's desire.

ISAIAH 48

17 *Thus says the Lord, your Redeemer, the Holy One of Israel:
I am the Lord your God who teaches you to profit, Who
leads you by the way that you should go.*

18 *Oh, that you had harkened to My commandments! Then your
peace and prosperity would have been like a flowing river;
and your righteousness [the holiness and purity of the
nation] like the abundant waves of the sea; (Amplified)*

God prospered Abraham, Joseph, Joshua, and many other people in the Bible. Their prosperity included wealth, and riches, and often money. The opposite of financial prosperity is poverty. Poverty, or absence of prosperity, is a curse as listed in the curses that would come upon people when they took themselves out from under God's protection through disobedience. (Deuteronomy 28:29).

PROVERBS 10

15 *The rich man's wealth is his strong city; the poverty of the poor is their ruin. (Amplified)*

A "just enough" mentality falls in this category as well. Having just enough is basically selfishness, as you are limited in being able to bless others by giving. God wants overflow in our lives so that we can bless others and be a financial pipeline for the Kingdom of God.

LUKE 4

18 *The Spirit of the Lord [is] upon Me, because He has anointed me [the anointed One, the Messiah] to preach the good news (the Gospel) to the poor; he has sent Me to announce release to the captives, and recovery of sight to the blind; to send forth delivered those who are oppressed— who are downtrodden, bruised, crushed and broken down by calamity; (Amplified)*

Note that for each problem Jesus prescribed an opposite. Jesus brought the solution. Blind— see; oppressed— delivered; captives— freed; and the poor— have the Gospel preached to them. For what purpose? To remove them from their poverty! Some will ask, "Did not Jesus say that the poor will always be with us?" Answer, yes, but why? Simply not all will believe the Gospel, which is the power of God unto salvation. Salvation in every realm of life!

WHY GOD WANTS TO BLESS HIS PEOPLE

There are at least four reasons why God wants to bless us. The primary meaning of the Hebrew word "to bless" is to be empowered to prosper. As we have seen, God certainly wants to empower His people to prosper. Here are four reasons why:

1) Reason number one: God prospers us simply because we are His children.

MATTHEW 7

9 *Or what man is there of you, if his son asks him for a loaf of bread, will hand him a stone?*

10 *Or if he asks for a fish, will hand him a serpent?*

11 *If you then, evil as you are, know how to give good and advantageous gifts to your children, how much more will your Father Who is in heaven [perfect as He is] give good and advantageous things to those who keep on asking Him! (Amplified)*

God's desire is to give good gifts to His children. A good gift would be the absence of poverty, for example. Some people think God wants to keep us poor to keep us humble! This is not God's way of developing humility. You would not wish that on your children; why would God?

God has purpose for prosperity. It is not to be an end in itself. God has revealed Himself as Jehovah Jireh— our provider or literally, "Jehovah's provision shall be seen." The focus must be on God, Himself, as our source. Many have made the mistake of making prosperity an end in itself. This then makes money the end and God the means, rather than God being the end and money the means. Thus when God is the end, we can discover His purpose in prosperity.

Some people have a major resistance to the teaching of prosperity because of how prosperity sometimes was used— to heap on oneself. Some have focused on what they could get. However, we don't want to throw the baby out with the bath water! We must always keep the baby and get rid of the bath water! Prosperity must be taught in the context of having a closed circle, or a budget in which one has answered the question, "How much is enough?" Without God's answer to that question, the Mammon spirit will influence one's mind and heart concerning prosperity, and the prosperity God provides, will be misused. We must be rightly taught about money and the Mammon system behind it.

Another influence in our thinking comes from the world system and its classical teaching on economics (for more detail, see the next section on Treasures in Heaven). Many people have a zero-sum or pie concept of wealth. They assume that the wealth in the world is a fixed value. Therefore, in order to increase your piece of the pie, you must take from another person, thus making it impossible for them to have wealth also. The truth is that wealth is in abundance, and value is created by diligence in work and creative ideas. The ebb and flow of finances in the earth are based on God's covenants with mankind, and man's ability to understand and walk in these covenants.

DEUTERONOMY 8

18   But you shall (earnestly) remember the Lord your God; for it is He Who gives you power to get wealth *that He may establish His covenant* which He swore to your fathers, as at this day. (Amplified)

All wealth originally comes from God, and only those who are in covenant with Him have a right to possess and utilize it.

PROVERBS 13

22b ...and the wealth of the sinner [finds it way eventually] into the hands of the righteous, for whom it was laid up. (Amplified)

We must come into a position of financial stewardship so that the Lord can trust us with such a release to bless and serve the Kingdom of God! Thus, your prosperity is not at the expense of other people! God is able to provide prosperity for all people. However, there are conditions to be met. We must walk in obedience to God's laws that govern prosperity. Man has sinned and abused his God-given purpose for being blessed and being a blessing to others. He/she has selfishly heaped upon himself/herself and abused prosperity. That misuse does not limit God's desire to prosper His children!

2) **Reason number two. Prosperity is meant to free us from the care of things.**

The world system defines prosperity differently than it is defined in the Kingdom. This system tells us that prosperity is the having and acquiring of more things. I (Earl) saw a bumper sticker, which said: "He who dies with the most toys, wins!" This is a sad statement of the affairs of the world system. God's heart is to prosper us so that our closed circle or budget is met and there is overflow that bounces off the circle to bless others and finance the activities of the Kingdom of God, not to feed the insatiable desires of human selfishness.

DEUTERONOMY 8

17 And beware lest you say in your [mind and] heart, My power and the might of my hand have gotten me this wealth. (Amplified)

The enemy can and may release riches (money that works for you) to people to divert their attention away from God our provider. If these people do not understand God's purpose for prosperity, they may squander it on themselves. With only an open circle, they can increase the size of their circle, without consulting the Lord, and interpret this increase as God's blessing. Without a closed circle and answering the question "How much is enough?," prosperity can be a snare.

There are two types of "cares." Having too little is a care, because we are then hindered from doing what God has called us to do. Much time is spent trying to "make money." Having too much is also a care, because we then have to look after all the "stuff." It has to be protected, maintained, and properly managed, which takes time and more resources. The care of things can be a burden. What is the balance? It is different for each person. Only God knows what the size our circle is to be for the work He has called us to do. We must seek and be in agreement with the Lord over what is in our circle. God has principles, commandments and an opinion on everything else!

Some people have a poverty mentality. These people think that humility is living with just enough to barely meet their own obligations and necessities. They have no concept of managing an abundant supply of resources with which to bless others. Other people can be in presumption, thinking God wants them to have more than enough just to satisfy hidden greed or make a value statement to other people by what they own. The point is, we must have a closed circle that covers Obligations, Necessities and Wants, with God in agreement in each of these categories. We then can be trusted by the Lord to be good stewards in the managing of our closed circle and then the overflow that God wants to bring to us for Kingdom purposes. (We will cover in more detail in chapter six how to close the circle and become a manager of God's resources.)

3) Reason number three. Prosperity is meant to empower us to be generous to others.

A key principle in the Kingdom of God is giving. God wants financial prosperity in our lives so we are able to give.

2 CORINTHIANS 9

7 *Let each one [give] as he has made up his own mind and
purposed in his heart, not reluctantly or sorrowfully or under
compulsion, for God loves (that is, He takes pleasure in,
prizes above other things, and is unwilling to abandon or to
do without) a cheerful (joyous, prompt-to-do-it) giver— whose
heart is in his giving. (Amplified)*

That certainly covers it! We can give in many arenas, such as
time, talents and service, but a major area of giving is in finances. If
we have no money, we can't be generous to others around us. Thus, a
major reason why God wants to prosper us is to make it possible for
us to simply be generous to those around us. Giving can be done
from our closed circle as we make funds available by shifting them
from a particular category into giving. In any given month we can
decide to take some money from one or more categories and give it
rather than spend it on items in that grouping. Giving can also come
from our overflow, funds that are over and above our closed circle
budget. However, we want our giving to be directed by the Lord, not
by guilt or misguided mercy. Some people give out of guilt for over-
spending. Others may give out of fear or even because of the
pressure of manipulation. The Lord wants to prompt us to give and
be available to Him to financially meet specific needs.

4) Reason number four. Prosperity is meant to empower us to fund world evangelism.

It is going to take billions of dollars to complete the Great
Commission. However, there are already sufficient funds in the
hands of Christians to complete the assignment. Many times these
finances are buried in the world system, working for percentage
increases, rather than receiving multiplication increase through Kingdom usage. Money given for Kingdom use has a way to make us
active in many places at once. Giving to mission projects world-wide
makes us in a sense "omnipresent." We can direct money to be
working all over the world at once, whereas you and I can be in only

one place at a time. When there is overflow financially in our lives, we can use the money to force the world system to do work for the Kingdom of God. With money we can print bibles, travel anywhere in the world, build churches and be involved in all types of mercy ministries in the name of Jesus.

Biblical prosperity will work in any nation and culture on the planet. Kingdom principles of finance will work in any culture when a person operates by faith and becomes a doer of the Word. Jesus taught biblical finances in a third world nation. Israel at that time was an occupied nation, under the rule of the Romans. Their own currency had been outlawed except in the temple, and Roman currency was forced into circulation. Economically they were in bondage to the Romans.

Let us consider how Jesus dealt with the finances necessary for His ministry. There is no record of Jesus' praying for finances. In His ministry, Judas was the treasurer. Judas was responsible for the distribution of money to the poor and buying things for the ministry. We know that Judas was a thief and regularly stole from the money box. How long would your ministry or business function today if you had a thief for a treasurer? Yet Jesus' ministry never lacked!

JOHN 12

4   *But Judas Iscariot, the one of His disciples who was about to betray Him, said,*

5   *'Why was this perfume not sold for three hundred denarii (the wages of an ordinary workman for a whole year), and that given to the poor— the destitute?' (Amplified)*

Where did Judas get this idea? I am sure he heard Jesus say this to the rich young ruler and thought that was a good line!

JOHN 12

6   *Now he did not say this because he cared for the poor, but because he was a thief and having the bag [the moneybox,*

the purse of the twelve], he took for himself what was put into it— pilfering the collections. (Amplified)

How much was going into the box? We don't know, but it supported a thief's lifestyle and the ministry did not lack. I (Earl) have a theory about Judas, which I cannot prove from Scripture, but I think it is probably correct. Knowing that Judas was a thief, we could assume that if there were not a continual flow of finances from which to pilfer, Judas would have left the group and joined another ministry that could support his habit! However, Jesus never lacked finances to do what His Father had called him to do. In John 13, at the last supper, we find that the disciples were totally oblivious to the motives of Judas.

JOHN 13

29 Some thought that since Judas had the money box (the purse), Jesus was telling him, Buy what we need for the festival, or that he should give something to the poor. (Amplified)

Jesus was constantly giving to the poor and Kingdom principles were operative in His life. We observe that there was a constant supply of finances.

We also find in Scripture that prosperity is promised by God to:

1. Those who meditate in the Word of God. Psalm 1

2. Those who seek God. 2 Chronicles 26:5; 14:7

3. Those who are obedient. 1 Chronicles 22:12,13; Isaiah 1:19

4. Those who trust in Him. Jeremiah 17:7,8; 2 Chronicles 20:20

TREASURES IN HEAVEN

The study of economics in the world system of finance is very different from the study of finance in the Kingdom of God.

First of all, the word "economics" needs to be defined. The English word, economics, comes from the Greek word "oikonomia" meaning the "management of a household." So we can have household management according to biblical principles, thus biblical economics, or simply by world system economics. However, today there is another definition of economics. Paul Samuelson and William D. Nordhaus in their book *E conomics,*[5] define the word as follows: "Economics is the study of how people and society choose to employ <u>scarce resources</u> that could have alternative uses in order to produce various commodities and to distribute them for consumption." You will notice the phrase "scarce resources" is used in the definition. This type of thinking is governed by the world system. The Bible does not talk about scarcity of resource in the Kingdom of God, but rather of abundance. The Word always talks about increase, multiplication and prosperity in dealing with the biblical principles that govern the lives of Christians on Planet Earth. God's blessing on you and me is not at the expense of someone else. Thus, we need to have our minds renewed by the Word of God so that our thinking will not be that of managing scarce resource, but rather that of managing abundance and expecting increase in all areas of our lives. At times in the past we had thought to use the term "Kingdom Economics." However, with the above understanding, it is now evident that this would be an oxymoron. Consequently, we will talk about the Kingdom system of finances. Jesus introduces this Kingdom system of finances in the following Scripture.

MATTHEW 6

19 *Do not gather and heap up and store for yourselves treasures on earth, where moth and rust and worm consume and destroy, and where thieves break through and steal;*

20 *But gather and heap up and <u>store for yourselves Treasures in Heaven</u> where neither moth nor rust nor worm consume and destroy, and where thieves do not break through and steal;*

---

[5] Paul Samuelson and William D. Nordhaus, *E conomics* 12th edition, 1985, New York, (McGraw Hill), p.4

21 *For where your treasure is, there will your heart be also.*
(Amplified)

Now, treasures on earth are referring to various forms of securities, investments, savings accounts, etc. If you consider them to be "treasures," they are something that you prize, look to for security, and trust in; your heart (emotions) will become committed to these things, as treasures. The Word, tells us not to gather up treasures on earth, because the heart emotionally locks into these and trusts in them. In reality, this is idolatry (a trust in something or someone other than Jesus Christ). Now, the Word says not to gather up treasures on earth, because when the value of these investments suddenly declines such as in a stock market crash or hyper-inflation, such a person could be emotionally devastated. The world system controls the money in circulation. Money, as we have seen, is used as a medium of exchange, but has no actual value. The value of money is only a reflection of its purchasing power, which is determined by fickle markets. It is important not to have too much or too little of it around.

In the above Scripture, Jesus uses the analogy of moth, rust and worm. The moth, may be picturing inflation, a decline in the value of existing money as a result of having too much of it in circulation. In actuality, the rate of increase of the investments of many people does not even keep pace with the rate of inflation. The rust may be picturing deflation, an increase in the value of existing money due to having too little money in circulation. This results in an economic slowdown or even brings commerce to a halt. The worm may be picturing international devaluation, which affects many people in countries that have currency tied to the U.S. dollar, or other foreign currencies. Then, Jesus said that thieves break through and steal. This could be referring to the uncertainty of all the investment markets, both bulls and bears. The thief may also be referring to fraud, collapses of financial institutions, such as the Savings and Loans in the United States in the 1980s, bank failures, financial market collapses, and fraudulent investment schemes.

If you trust in these things and treasure them for security in the future, you will certainly be disappointed. We all have heard stories of people in 1929 who jumped from buildings when there was a severe downturn in the U.S. stock market. Of course, there are also untold stories of people who, upon experiencing a financial reversal, get caught up in drugs, affairs, gambling, crime and other activities which before would have been totally out of character. Is it wrong then to have investments in the World System? No, of course not. However, to put treasure in investments is wrong. When your investments have you, then they become "treasure" to you, and your heart (emotions) becomes tied to the world system of finances.

Jesus instructed us to gather up for ourselves Treasures in Heaven, where these problems do not exist and where our hearts would be safe to be associated with these treasures. God has created us such that our hearts will naturally pursue whatever we perceive to be treasure (verse 21). Consequently, He wants us to have our treasure in the right place, so that our hearts will pursue that which truly has value. The economic system of the world, with all its problems and scarcities, does not affect our "Treasures in Heaven." Thus, we must learn to do what Jesus told us in the imperative tense, when He said (I command you to) "gather and heap up and store for yourself treasure in heaven." Because the Lord has a large vision for our lives, Jesus knew that we would have need of much money during our lifetime, to fulfill God's plan. Therefore, He outlined for us His Kingdom financial system that provides increase and multiplication, which is not limited by inflation, deflation, devaluation or thievery.

God wants us to know His ways as Moses sought to know God's ways (Exodus 39:13). In the Matthew 6:19-34, Jesus teaches us Kingdom principles of finances. He says this only after He has given us the solution in verse 20. That is why verse 25 starts off with the word, "Therefore." This word links verse 25 to the passage immediately preceding it. (Whenever you see a "therefore" in the Bible, it is good to find out what it is there for.) God's heart for us is so loving, not wanting us to perish in any area of our lives, that He has left us a record of over 2,000 verses to guide us financially! What do we have to do to obey the command of verse 20?

Let us revisit again the passage, which entails Jesus' encounter with the rich, young ruler (as is subtitled in some Bible translations). Jesus tells us here how to lay up for ourselves Treasures in Heaven.

MARK 10

21 *A nd Jesus, looking upon him loved him, and He said to him, 'You lack one thing; go and sell all you have, and give [the money] to the poor, and you will have treasure in heaven; and come [and] accompany Me— walking the same road that I walk.'*

22 *A t that saying the man's countenance fell and was gloomy, and he went away grieved and sorrowing, for he was holding great possessions. (A mplified)*

Notice that Jesus discerns that this young man's treasure is in his riches, and he is ensnared by the Mammon spirit. Thus, he was not able to be obedient to do what Jesus instructed. Jesus loved him and wanted him free, so Jesus told him how to obtain his freedom. He was to convert all the possessions and riches into money and GIVE it away! In this way, he would profane Mammon, which is to take away its power and ability to be worshipped. Notice that Jesus did not leave him without financial understanding of the Kingdom, as He said "and you will have Treasure In Heaven." Jesus had hoped to establish this young man in Kingdom principles of finance. He knew that when the young man obeyed and gave whenever Jesus told him to, his giving would be deposited or, credited to his heavenly account as treasure in heaven. Unfortunately, this young man declined the opportunity, as the paradigm shift was too great for him to comprehend. The Mammon spirit held control over his heart and mind, for he went away grieved and sorrowing.

TREASURES IN HEAVEN ACCOUNT

Dr	Cr

We need to think of Treasures in Heaven as an account with debits and credits. We can make deposits into this account, and we can withdraw from it. This is not unlike an account in an earthly bank. However, this account is not subject to the problems of earthly banks. Jesus knew that the wealthy, young man would need a source of finances for the future, and He wanted him free to follow Him. Jesus knew that a trust in the world system of finances would retain the young man in slavery.

Earthly accounts in banks traditionally pay interest at a very low percentage rate. However, the Treasures in Heaven account multiplies, as does everything in which God is involved. God's command to Adam and Eve was to be fruitful and multiply. God's original purpose was for multiplication. The two parables of Jesus in Matthew 25:14-29 and Luke 19:13-26, deal with the stewardship of money. In both of these parables, Jesus commended the servants who multiplied what was entrusted to them. There was a two-time multiplication in Matthew 25, a 10- and 5-time multiplication mentioned in Luke 19. We believe that our heavenly account multiplies. There is always a greater account balance than simply what we deposited. Jesus watches over our account, instructing us when and where to give, placing deposits in our heavenly account for Him to multiply.

MARK 12

41 *Now Jesus sat opposite the treasury and saw how the people put money into the treasury. And many who were rich put in much.*

42 *Then one poor widow came and threw in two mites, which make a quadrans.*

43 *So He called His disciples to Himself and said to them, 'Assuredly, I say to you that this poor widow has put in more than all those who have given to the treasury.*

44 *For they all put in out of their abundance, but she out of her poverty (want -KJV) put in all that she had, her whole livelihood.' (NKJV)*

Jesus sat watching this event and made comments to His disciples about giving. Certainly Jesus had been teaching His disciples the Kingdom system of finances. The widow lady gave out of her want. She understood the concept of treasures in heaven and how God's method of supply through giving operated. Now Jesus was in the earthly temple observing front row, center all that was being given. We know that the earthly temple is modeled after the real one, which is in heaven itself, (Hebrews 9:24). Now Jesus has already entered into heaven and the heavenly temple. No longer is the type of shadow necessary. We have the real thing. Jesus has now taken His place in heaven and is overseeing our heavenly account. He is interested in our deposits and takes delight in our obedience to give as He instructs us. Deposits are made when we give as the Lord instructs us. Not all giving is instructed by Him. Some people give out of guilt, or fear or a desire to get. We should ask the Lord if we are to give, and if so how much.

The apostle Paul was taught by Jesus and thus was able to teach Timothy Kingdom principles of finances. In his letter, Paul instructs Timothy regarding rich men and how they are to relate to their riches.

1 TIMOTHY 6

17 *A s for the rich in this world, charge them not to be proud and arrogant and contemptuous of others, nor to set their hopes on uncertain riches but on God, who richly and ceaselessly provides us with everything for [our] enjoyment.*

18 *[Charge them] to do good, to be rich in good works, to be liberal and generous-hearted ready to share [with others],*

19 *In this way laying up for themselves [the riches that endure forever] a good foundation for the future, so that they may grasp that which is life indeed. (Amplified)*

Now let's examine these verses. You will remember that we have defined riches as money that is working for you. Riches, like money, are distinguished from wealth, and abide under the influence of the Mammon spirit. This spirit wants us to trust in riches and see them as our source, especially for the future. Paul warns rich people not to be proud and arrogant, or as the King James Version states, not to be high minded, nor trust in uncertain riches. Moth, rust, worms and thieves will frequently depreciate the value of riches carried in the heart as treasures on earth. Instead, Paul instructs the rich to put their trust in God, Who provides everything for our enjoyment. The Greek word for "everything" means just that, everything!

Subsequently, in verse 18, Paul commands the rich to do good and be generous and liberal in their giving. The result is seen in verse 19. The New English Bible states, **"and so acquire a treasure which will form a good foundation for the future."** Paul knew that we would need finances in the future and so to lay the foundation in Kingdom finances, we are to give when the Lord instructs us and this amount is then credited in our heavenly account. Inflation, deflation, devaluation, and financial scams do not affect our heavenly account. As a result, our heavenly account is a place in which our hearts can safely find rest and peace. Notice that verse 19 in the Amplified version states, "the riches that endure forever," in other words, not affected by the world system, a good foundation for the future. People are looking for some form of investment that will be a good foundation financially for the future. Paul states that our giving is just that foundation for the future financially. Then we grasp "that which is life indeed!" In other words, with our hearts at rest, we can get on with that which God is calling us to do. Our focus will not be on working to "make a living," but rather on working to "make a giving" (Ephesians 4:28). We also see this same principle of finances taught here by Paul to Timothy.

In Philippians 4:14-19, Paul is writing to the believers at Philippi and instructing them on finances. Verse 19 is very familiar to most Christians. We have frequently heard it quoted when offerings are received. However, verse 19 is actually not a stand-alone verse, but rather is the conclusion of process outlined in the preceding passage.

PHILIPPIANS 4

14   But it was right and commendable and noble of you to contribute for my needs and to share my difficulties with me.

15   And you Philippians yourselves will know that in the early days of the Gospel ministry, when I left Macedonia, no church (assembly) entered into partnership with me and opened up [a debit and credit] account in giving and receiving except you only.

16   For even in Thessalonica you sent [me contributions] for my needs, not only once but a second time.

17   Not that I seek or am eager for [your] gift, but I do seek and am eager for the fruit which increases to your credit— the harvest of blessing that is accumulating to your account. (Amplified)

The understanding in the Greek text expanded in English in the Amplified version makes it very clear how Kingdom finances should be considered. Giving, as instructed by the Lord, opens up a debit and credit account in giving and receiving. Paul then encouraged the Philippians to keep on giving. This was not for his sake but rather for their own sakes, as their giving would be accumulating and multiplying in their accounts. We see him here again describe the concept of Treasures in Heaven. Paul knew that they would have need of finances in the future and that by crediting their account in the present, there would then be plenty in the account for future withdrawal.

PHILIPPIANS 4

18   But I have [your full payment] and more; I have everything I need and am amply supplied, now that I have received from Epaphroditus the gifts you sent me. [They are the] fragrant odor [of] an offering and sacrifice which God welcomes and in which He delights.

19 And my God will liberally supply (fill to the full) your every need according to His riches in glory in Christ Jesus. (Amplified)

How can Paul be so emphatic with the Philippians, that God will supply their every need? He does this with total confidence, because he understands Sparrow Faith and he knows that they have laid up for themselves significant Treasures in Heaven. They will be able to withdraw from that heavenly account. God is their source, and Kingdom principles of finance are at work!

In the book of Acts we find the story of Cornelius and his encounter with an angel of God. It is very interesting to notice what God has remembered about Cornelius. The Bible records that God had taken notice of Cornelius' prayers and his giving to the poor.

ACTS 10

4 And he, gazing intently at him became frightened, and said, 'What is it, Lord'? And the angel said to him, 'Your prayers and your [generous] gifts to the poor have come up [as a sacrifice] to God and have been remembered by Him'. (Amplified)

We know how to deposit in our heavenly account, by giving when the Lord prompts us to give. It is obedience, not fear, guilt, or compulsion that credits the giving to our account. Now how do we withdraw from our account when we have need of finances? In the natural realm, when we go to the bank, there is a procedure that we must follow in order to withdraw money. So it is with our heavenly account. We know that God responds not to need, but rather to faith. The Word states that without faith it is impossible to please Him (Hebrews 11:6a). Thus, faith is a basic requirement in dealing with our heavenly account. We must ask in faith, believing. In John 16, we find Jesus teaching his disciples this principle.

JOHN 16

23 *And when that time comes, you will ask nothing of Me— you will need to ask Me no questions. I assure you, most solemnly I tell you, that My Father will grant you whatever you ask in My name. (Amplified)*

Most versions of the Bible translate this last phrase as, "My Father will give you whatever you ask in My name." However, the Greek word translated "give" would be better translated utilizing the English word "grant." Today when we talk of "grants," we think more in terms of money that is released to people who have made application for funding, and are subsequently given a "grant."

When we think of the release of finances from our heavenly account, it is released on the basis of asking in faith, and believing, without wavering. **This is the application procedure for obtaining the grant.** We need to ask specifically for our financial grants, not just, "I need money!" This requires the elements of good stewardship and planning in the financial area. We are already aware that we are dealing in the spirit realm when it comes to finances. Release of finances into the hands of Christians requires money belonging to the world system to be pressed into service to accomplish a Kingdom purpose.

When such person is a steward of "that which belongs to another" (Luke 16:12), and has an operating Treasures in Heaven account, he/she can then apply for a grant according to Mark 11:23-24. God will require money to be released from the world system into the hands of the one who has met God's higher order principles governing money.

MARK 11

23 *Truly, I tell you, whoever says to this mountain, Be lifted up and thrown into the sea and does not doubt at all in his heart, but believes that what he says will take place, it will be done for him.*

24 For this reason I am telling you, whatever you ask for in prayer, believe— trust and be confident— that it is granted to you and you will [get it]. (Amplified)

Notice again the word "granted" in verse 24. We have confidence in God's releasing this grant, because we first of all understand Sparrow Faith. Provision of our basic needs is guaranteed because our Father in heaven loves us. So as we prepare our budget, planning ahead, we are in a place to ask God specifically for an amount to meet our daily or weekly or monthly "bread," in faith knowing that as we pray in faith, we will receive this grant.

Secondly, we are all called to live by faith. However this is not blind faith with no basis behind it. We understand that we have an account in heaven that Jesus oversees called a "Treasures in Heaven account." If we have made deposits in this account through our giving, then this account will have more than enough in it to meet any additional requests. This principle is applicable to all Christians in all walks of life. Some have a mind-set that this applies only to missionaries and evangelists who "live by faith" or to those who are out of work or don't have enough to meet their monthly needs. This thinking again indicates a trust in an employer, or our self-employed work as the source of provision. If we have a job, we must understand that the employer or the job is not our source. Now God delegates employers to pay our salaries, but He alone is at all times the source. Our basic needs are met through Sparrow Faith, and our Treasures in Heaven account is then available for financing all other requests.

Let me (Earl) give you an example from my own life. I was employed by IBM, for 19 years. When God called my wife, me and our family to join Youth With A Mission, I remember the day I received my last paycheck from the company. There was no fear or anxiety because we knew that God was our source. We realized that nothing was really changing. All that would happen was that God would delegate or use other means to release money into our hands. The money is on the earth, but the accounting is done in heaven! I had settled it beforehand that IBM was not my source, but delegated by God to pay my salary! God was my employer and my source. If a company goes bankrupt or your job is lost because of the economic downturns of the world system, then God can open up some other employment opportunities where He can delegate others as a channel of provision for you. Your heavenly account is always intact regardless of what happens on the earth. That is why it is so important for us to operate in Kingdom principles of finance.

Another question that may still be in your mind is, "How do the finances come to us?" "What is God's channel and place of provision?" In Chapter two we talked about the fact that God has many ways of getting money into our hands. Now let's talk about three different ways that God may provide.

The first is called "manna provision." Just as God provided manna to His people in the wilderness, God can get provision to His children today. We love to read "manna" stories. Whether it be from the life of George Muller in England, where daily food and money came miraculously to feed the orphans and build housing, or modern-day stories in the lives of Christians all over the world. We are all thrilled by this manner of God's provision.

The second way is through a harvest for which you have not worked. When the children of Israel crossed the Jordan river, the manna stopped and provision came through a harvest that they had not planted. Their job was to harvest what others had sown. This harvest may come through inheritances, or specific giving of others as a blessing to you and your family.

The third way God may provide is through specific seed that God puts in your hands as work to be done that will provide employment, or investment. After reaping the harvest they found in Canaan, the Israelites were required to sow for their harvest in the next season. When we are walking with God, our work should be blessed (Haggai 2:19). God wants us to be aware that we will be more fruitful on our jobs when our lives are dedicated to Him. It may be an idea that God gives you which, when developed, starts a business or service which will reap financially and provide for your needs. Following the leading of God's spirit in contacting people, making yourself available for an opportunity, applying yourself in study or at a job, opens doors for advancement and increased remuneration. God is constantly putting something in our minds, hearts, and hands on which to follow through. There are two complementary forces that come to bear on our financial prosperity. The first is the confession or the mouth in agreement with God, and the second is the diligence of the hands.

PROVERBS 12

14 From the fruit of his words, a man shall be satisfied with good, and the work of a man's hands shall come back to him [as a harvest]. (Amplified)

We need both faith confession and work. Faith confession without works will be superficial and lack the perseverance to bring true prosperity. On the other hand, the work ethic without the spiritual power of faith confession will limit grace and anointing to bring about all the financial prosperity that God intends for us. To combine faith and diligence, we will be operating under God's covenant to receive His full blessings. God has ways of providing promotion, and raises, and increase above the norm when we operate in diligence and excellence.

In Matthew 6 after Jesus explains Treasures in Heaven, He goes on in verses 25 through 34 instructing us not to be anxious or worried in the area of finances. Jesus told us rather to seek first the Kingdom of God and His righteousness and all these other things will be granted unto us. Five times we are exhorted not to worry or be anxious over finances or what finances will buy (vs. 25, 27, 28, 31 & 34). Jesus did not just say, "Don't worry," but told us what we need to know, so our heart will be at peace and rest. We are told to seek first His Kingdom and His righteousness and specifically in this chapter, that His method of financial multiplication is to heap and store for ourselves Treasures in Heaven. It is critical for us as believers to know how His system works and have it in operation. In this way, God is our source, rather than our looking to our job or the world's system. Then worry and anxiety over finances will have no place in us, as we are established in His truth.

Hosea 4:6 warns us that God's people are destroyed for lack of knowledge. In Proverbs 5:23 the Scripture tells us that the wicked man will die for lack of discipline and instruction, and in the greatness of his folly will he go astray and be lost. Thus, it is critical for us to understand and operate in God's principles of finance. Some say, "Oh, these principles will work only in a wealthy western nation." No, these financial principles work in any culture or country in the world. Jesus, Himself, lived and taught these principles in Israel, which was at that time a "third world" nation.

PART TWO:
FIVE BIBLICAL USES OF MONEY

SEEK WISDOM NOT FORMULAS

As we look at five different biblical uses of money, we believe that it is critical not only to know what to do, but to know why to do it. King Solomon was a man who prospered tremendously financially as King of Israel. His father, David, taught him not only what to do but why to do it. In the latter years of his life, David prayed for his son, Solomon, for wisdom and understanding.

1 CHRONICLES 22

11 Now, my son, may the Lord be with you; and may you prosper, and build the house of the Lord your God, as He has said to you.

12 Only may the Lord give you wisdom and understanding, and give you charge concerning Israel, that you may keep the law of the Lord your God.

13 Then you will prosper, if you take care to fulfill the statutes and judgments with which the Lord charged Moses concerning Israel. Be strong and of good courage; do not fear nor be dismayed. (NKJV)

Wisdom and understanding are far more valuable than formulas of what to do. Many people simply try to use formulas designed by others without the wisdom or understanding behind the formulas. This almost always produces disaster and disappointment. I (Craig) have run into many Christians who tell me, "I tried all those things that prosperity teachers teach and it didn't work." This lets me know right away that such a person did not receive the understanding and wisdom behind what was taught, but merely attempted to follow someone's external formulas.

Solomon prospered because he not only received his father's formulas, but because he sought the wisdom of his father's God. The result in Solomon's life was prosperity that came through the wisdom and understanding of the principles.

2 CHRONICLES 1

7   On that night God appeared to Solomon, and said to him, 'Ask! What shall I give you?'

8   And Solomon said to God: 'You have shown great mercy to David my father, and have made me king in his place.

9   Now, O Lord God, let Your promise to David my father be established, for You have made me king over a people like the dust of the earth in multitude.

10 <u>Now give me wisdom and knowledge</u>, that I may go out and come in before this people; for who can judge this great people of Yours?'

11 Then God said to Solomon: 'Because this was in your heart, and you have not asked riches or wealth or honor or the life of your enemies, nor have you asked long life- but have asked wisdom and knowledge for yourself, that you may judge My people over whom I have made you king,

12 wisdom and knowledge are granted to you; and I will give you riches and wealth and honor, such as none of the kings have had who were before you nor shall any after you have the like.' (NKJV)

I believe that Solomon asked God for wisdom and under-standing, because his father, David, taught him to do so and prayed the same for him. God's response was that He not only gave Solomon the wisdom and understanding, but also riches, wealth and honor. Each of us would do well to not seek God for wealth, but rather for wisdom and understanding. As we look at five biblical uses of money, ask the Lord to give you not only an external formula, but rather the wisdom and understanding behind the principle.

Let us now look specifically at five biblical uses of money. We have learned that money is not to be our master, but rather our servant (slave), subject to our control. When we recognize that money is impotent, then we are free from its pursuit and can press it into service to do Kingdom work. What then are legitimate uses for money? We believe that we can find five legitimate uses for money outlined by Paul in 2 Corinthians 9:8-11.

2 CORINTHIANS 9

8 *A nd God is able to make all grace (every favor and earthly blessing) come to you in abundance, so that you may always and under all circumstances and whatever the need, be self-sufficient— possessing enough to require no aid or support and furnished in abundance for every good work and charitable donation.*

9 *As it is written, He (the benevolent person) scatters abroad, he gives to the poor; his deeds of justice and goodness and kindness and benevolence will go on and endure forever!*

10 *A nd God Who provides seed for the sower and bread for eating will also provide and multiply your (resources for) sowing, and increase the fruits of your righteousness (which manifests itself in active goodness, kindness and charity).*

11 *Thus you will be enriched in all things and in every way, that you can be generous, (and your generosity as it is) administered by us will bring forth thanksgiving to God. (A mplified)*

Firstly, we see here in verse eight that God is able to make all grace abound toward us. The phrase "is able" shows us that it is not automatic. There are conditions to be met. The primary requirement to receiving God's grace is faith toward God. So Sparrow Faith is the primary requirement for receiving God's grace. The primary hindrance to Sparrow Faith is attempting to get God to meet our needs based on our works. As we become secure in Sparrow Faith, we continually receive our provision as a gift from God rather than something we are owed as a result of our work. By God's grace, then, it is His pleasure to see to it that we always have all sufficiency in all things.

I (Craig) love it when God uses superlatives such as all and always. This represents His desire for us. He wants this to be true always. It is simply a matter of our receiving His grace. He then makes available an abundance to release prosperity in our lives for specific purposes. As we mentioned earlier, many Christians have been put off by the word "prosperity" because of the way it has been defined by certain segments of the body of Christ. I (Craig) would like to provide here another definition of prosperity. I believe that prosperity could be defined as enough of God's supply to accomplish God's instructions. Again, where there is no vision, there is no need for provision. He wants to prosper us and give us abundance for every good work for specific Kingdom purposes.

Here is a summary of the five different uses for money that we have seen in verses ten and eleven of Second Corinthians, chapter nine.

1. **Seed for the sower (Tithe)**
2. **Bread for eating (Consumption)**
3. **Multiplication of seed for sowing (Sowing and Reaping)**
4. **Increasing your fruits of righteousness (Using money to free people from bondage)**
5. **Generosity (Giving)**

Most people think that they have an understanding of number 1, know something about numbers 2, and 5, but know little to nothing about numbers 3 and 4. Each of these five uses of money has a different purpose in God's Kingdom and yields a different result. This above list contains legitimate uses for money. One obvious point is that we would not be able to use money for any of these purposes if we had no money available. Thus when God, Who is our source, makes money available, then these are ways that we should plan to use it. (It is interesting to note that paying interest on debt is not listed among these uses). Let us now look in more detail at each of these uses.

CHAPTER 4
SEED FOR THE SOWER

JOHN 4:23-24

SPIRIT	TRUTH
Faith *Romans 10:17* **Word**	Faith *Luke 17:5-10* **Obedience**
GRACE	**BUILDING BLOCKS**
2 CORINTHIANS 9:8	1. RECOGNIZE AND RENOUNCE THE SPIRIT OF MAMMON
And God is able to make all grace (every favor and earthly blessing) come to you in abundance, so that you may always and under all circumstances and whatever the need, be self sufficient, possessing enough to require no aid or support and furnished in abundance for every good work and charitable donation. (Amplified)	(Heart allegiance goes to God alone)
	2. ESTABLISH SPARROW FAITH
	(God is my source)
	3. ESTABLISH THE TITHE
	(Be a tither rather than just tithing)

The first usage of money, "seed for the sower," we consider to be the Tithe. This is the first thing we are to do with money. We are to give or return to God that which belongs to Him before we use money for anything else. As we look at this aspect of tithing, let us first start with answering some simple questions such as what, where, when, why, and how.

WHAT: The word tithe simply comes from the Hebrew word *"maaser,"* which means ten percent. Can one tithe 12%? No! Can one tithe 8%? No! One can tithe only ten percent (10%) because the meaning of the word is 10%. Thus, one cannot tithe 5% or any number other than 10%. Therefore, to tithe is simply to manage ten percent of the gross income available to you on behalf of the Lord. The issue of tithing on net or gross comes up if we don't understand the operation of the Mammon spirit. The goal is not to preserve more for myself, but rather to simply manage that which God says is His. Since He is the source of my provision, there is no question about my needs being met. Tithing is actually an act of spiritual warfare as we return to God His portion.

The way the tithe is calculated may be somewhat different depending on how income is received. If your primary channel of income is through employment, and you receive a regular paycheck, then your tithe is simply calculated as 10% of your gross wage. If you are self-employed or are a business owner, you may not receive a regular wage, but rather compensate yourself with the profit of your business. In this case, your tithe should be calculated as 10% of the profit, or the increase of your business. If a business makes only a 7% gross profit, and the owner gives 10% of the gross receipts (turnover) as a tithe, he will experience a net loss of 3% every month. This business owner will not continue to be in business very long if he continues this practice.

I (Craig) have a friend who is a dairy farmer, and has a wonderful heart for God. The Lord convicted him that he had not been tithing as he should, so he repented and began to give a tithe of the gross receipts of his dairy business. After a time, my friend noticed that his savings were depleting, and he was increasing the borrowing from his line of credit more each month. It wasn't long until his banker called him to account and helped him realize that his dairy business made less than a 10% profit. The banker helped my friend to realize that he was meant to give as a tithe 10% of the profit from his dairy business, not 10% of the gross receipts or turnover of the business.

Sometimes people who are generating money through real estate or investments have some difficulty calculating their tithe in that they never actually receive the profit as cash, but rather roll their profit over into a new investment. The goal here would be to calculate the actual profit on each transaction and give 10% of the calculated profit as a tithe.

While we are talking about what the tithe is, let us also talk a little about what the tithe is not. Tithing is not the solution to all your financial problems. Well-meaning Christians have told some, "If you will just start tithing, your financial problems will be solved." Tithing is not the answer to your financial problems. Again, many people have simply tried to implement an external practice without understanding the wisdom behind the practice. Tithing is a right thing to do, but some Christians are trusting in the principle of tithing rather than trusting in God as their source. Relationship with and trust in Jesus Christ is the answer to your financial problems.

Tithing does not produce improved standing with God. God does not value or favor those who tithe above those who do not. Faith in the blood of Jesus Christ produces favor and right standing with God. If this is not true, then we are relying again on our own religious works to produce a right standing with God.

Tithing does not remove a financial curse. Tithing with the right attitude may prevent certain future financial destruction, while failure to tithe may have serious negative consequences in your future financial situation. However, tithing does not remove a curse. Many have been taught from Malachi 3:9-10 that if you don't tithe, you are cursed with a curse.

MALACHI 3

8 *'In what way have we robbed You?' In tithes and offerings.*

9 *You are cursed with a curse for you have robbed Me, even this whole nation.*

10 *Bring all the tithes into the storehouse, that there may be food in My house, (NKJV)*

In reality, you cannot remove any type of curse through any right action on your part. Only faith in the blood of Jesus Christ can and does remove a curse (Galatians 3:13-14). Application of His blood to the curse already upon you is necessary to remove it from you. What is this curse? God wants us to operate in His Kingdom principles of finance. When we fail to be a tither, we place ourselves at the mercy of the world system and what it can provide for us. That system is cursed, because it is under the control of Satan. Repentance from dead works (the world system) and faith in the blood of Jesus and in His provision will remove us from this cursed system.

WHERE: Malachi 3:10 does tell us to bring the tithe into "the storehouse." We believe that the storehouse is the local fellowship in which you are spiritually fed and pastored. We don't believe that the storehouse is referring to missions, television ministries, or the local Christian school your children attend. Your storehouse is that local fellowship in which there are people who know you, care for you, and to whom you have granted spiritual authority to pastor you.

WHEN: The tithe should be given when it is received. We believe that it should be given weekly or monthly depending on when it is received. As I mentioned above, if one generates income primarily from real estate or investment, so there is no regular income, the tithe should be calculated and given each time a transaction is completed, even if no money is actually received. I have noticed that if this is not done, many times people never do tithe on the increase of their investments.

WHY: This is one of the most critical issues. We will give significant time to consider the reason behind tithing. Again, as we mentioned at the beginning of this chapter it is at least equally important to gain understanding and wisdom regarding a principle, as it is to simply implement the practice. Thus, many Christians tithe, but at the same time defeat many of God's purposes in their tithing.

The first reason to tithe is because tithing is an Ancient Path (Jeremiah 6:16). Tithing releases God's supernatural power into your finances. Some people may say that tithing is a part of the Old Testament Law of Moses, and that as such, it is no longer pertinent to our lives. Actually, tithing is first encountered in the Bible in Genesis 14:20 when Abraham gave a tithe to Malchizadek, King of Salem. This predated the Law of Moses by about four hundred thirty years and is spoken of again in Hebrews 7:4-8. We believe that this principle of tithing is not pertinent to any specific time, nation or part of scripture. We believe that tithing is an Ancient Path. It is a universal principle, such as the physical principle of gravity. These types of principles respect no man or time. They are universal and work the same for everyone at any time. Gravity, like tithing, does not care whether you are old or young, male or female, American, European, African, Australian, or Asian. It works the same for everyone all the time.

Someone will say, "Well, we're under grace, so we don't have to abide by these Old Testament principles." That is true. You don't have to do anything. It is God's desire for you to be born again. However, it is your choice to receive Christ. Nobody can force you to do anything. There are just certain principles, which, when followed, are really beneficial to your life. Salvation's one of them. Your salvation will greatly benefit you in eternity. However, nobody is going to force you. You don't have to operate in it.

Here is another example. The Bible says that your life would be a lot better off if you didn't fornicate or commit adultery. That is really true. These things are so. Your life would be better off if you retained yourself in sexual purity. Sexual purity will help your life. God's purpose in His expression of these commandments is not to try to put some law on you or to restrict you. God knows that abiding by these principles is simply going to benefit your life. There are devastating consequences to the violation of basic life principles.

Your family will be a lot better off if you learn how to bless your children. The Bible tells you how and when to impart blessing to them. But you don't have to. Your life would be a whole lot better off if you learn how to take one day in seven as a Sabbath rest. Your body needs to rest. Some Christians say, "Oh, that's law, I don't have to do that." No, you don't have to do that. But again, we have heard numerous testimonies of people who discovered that principle, and now get far more work done in six working days than they used to in seven. This again is not a law. It is an Ancient Path.

Many times people consider such basic principles as law, which no longer needs to be heeded since we are under grace. We would be better served by changing in our minds the word law to the word principle. Because these laws (principles) such as honoring the Sabbath rest, tithing, blessing children, retaining sexual purity, are really like the law (principle) of gravity. This is also a law. Suppose some Christian said, "If that is law, then I don't have to abide by it. I'm in Christ, under grace, and thus set free from the law." We don't need to argue with such a person. If this is your belief, then we can just let you try out in practical experience your disregard for this law. We can simply watch your life and see how this strategy works out. No one will force you. You are perfectly free to step off tall buildings and cliffs on a regular basis. On the way down just let the Lord know that you're under grace now, so this law of gravity is not applicable to your life!

I give this example because I (Craig) have observed that many people today have grown up in families, in which, parents established for their children many arbitrary, meaningless rules and laws. Maybe your father commanded you, saying, "Thou shalt not wear blue shirts on Thursday." As a result, for all of your growing up years, you never wore a blue shirt on a Thursday. This was an immutable family law. Then when you came into your adulthood, you noticed that others wore blue shirts on a Thursdays, seemingly without consequence. So you thought to yourself, "I wonder why my father forbade that. Perhaps it was arbitrary with no real consequence for violation." And so with great fear and trepidation one day, you wear a blue shirt on a Thursday. No lightening bolts come out of the sky. Nothing adverse happens. Everything seems to be okay.

You decide that your father's command was nothing more than an arbitrary edict with no purpose and no consequence. After wearing blue shirts on multiple Thursdays without adverse consequence, your prior determination is confirmed. This was just an antiquated, arbitrary edict established by your father for some absolutely frivolous reason.

Many people, having had this experience in their own family, then apply the same reasoning to the Word of God. Such ones believe that the laws of God are simply antiquated, arbitrary edicts like many of the commands of their natural fathers. The concept is that God, like a natural father, punishes for violation of these arbitrary edicts. "You better do this or I'll punish you or I'll get you!" (i.e., "Your finances are cursed if you don't tithe.")

However, I have found that most of the commands in the Word of God, are not primarily directive, but rather are descriptive. God is not trying to direct our lives, but rather to describe basic principles by which life functions. For example, when God says, "Attention!! Gravity at work. Do not step off the cliff," He is not giving an arbitrary directive and threatening punishment for disobedience. No! He understands the principle of gravity and is trying to spare us from a very negative consequence of its violation. There is a reason behind this command.

God's command in this case is descriptive, not directive. God is saying, "Don't do this, but rather do this." Why? Because it will bless your life. It will benefit your life. Not, "Because I am God, so you obey, or I will punish you." Tithing is an Ancient Path, like gravity. You don't have to abide by it, but it will greatly benefit your life if you choose to. Tithing is not an arbitrary law. As we will discuss below, it is intended by God to generate Sparrow Faith in our hearts toward God. It brings us into the place of needing a miracle. Tithing releases the supernatural into our finances, because it is a universal Ancient Path.

We have spoken to many people who, when they looked at their financial situation with their natural minds, could not see any way that they could tithe and still continue to pay their bills. After implementing the practice of tithing with the right attitude and becoming a tither for a few months, they have consistently reported that after paying all their bills, the amount of money available to them on the 90% of their income is more than that of the 100% formerly. We have then asked, "How does it work? Are you making more than you did before? Are you spending less than before?" Consistently they answer, "I don't know how it works. I'm not making any more, nor consciously spending any less than before." They have released God's supernatural power into their finances by lining their ways up with God's Ancient Ways.

What are some other reasons God would want you to tithe? Does God need your money? No, of course not. God owns the cattle on 1,000 hills and has available infinite wealth (Psalm 50:10-13). God is not after your money. He is after your heart. We believe that tithing is the practical action we put with the faith statement, "God is my source of provision, and the spirit of Mammon has no power in my life."

Apostle James told us in James 2:26 *"For as the body without the spirit is dead, so faith without works is dead also."* Tithing is the practical action that goes with our faith in God as source. Thus, tithing is for you, not for God. God's purpose is not to get your money, but rather to generate in your heart Sparrow Faith toward Him as source. Tithing is God's regular method of doing so.

Another method of generating Sparrow Faith in your heart would be for God to bring you into abject poverty. In so doing, you could learn to trust God moment by moment for everything. This is the method the Lord used with George Muller in the eighteenth century to teach him faith. George Muller ran an orphanage in England with no visible means of support. Each morning when he woke, he had no idea how the orphans in his care would be fed that day. Each day God provided all the needs of the orphanage super-naturally. Someone would just happen to drop by some food or money that just suited what was needed for that day.

Each of us could also learn Sparrow Faith in this way. However, I believe that God's preferred method is through the tithe. Tithing requires faith for anyone. Very few people have an extra 10% of their income just sitting around. If you make $1,000 per month, giving that $100 is difficult. You need every dollar available for expenses. If you make $10,000 per month, giving the $1,000 is difficult, as $1,000 is a lot of money. If you make $100,000 per month, most people would struggle giving $10,000 per month to their local church. I (Earl) learned tithing from my father. When I was 12 and had my first paper route, my father placed in my hands a set of church envelopes. Each envelope had two pockets, one for tithe and the other for offerings. I learned to tithe ten cents a week. Then when the numbers grew, the principle had been established in my life.

Thus, regular, consistent tithing is God's preferred method of establishing Sparrow Faith in our hearts towards Him as our source. I believe that it is also God's method of establishing financial discipline in our lives. A person who has never established the discipline of tithing, rarely has the ability to exercise discipline in any other area of his/her financial life. The discipline of tithing is very similar to the discipline of fasting. A person who has no discipline of fasting in his or her life is usually undisciplined overall in relationship to food, and many other areas.

In the book of Malachi, we find that the prophet starts out proclaiming God's heart. In chapter 1, verse 2, he states, "I have loved you, says the Lord." That is God's position toward us. His commands are for our benefit.

Let us now look at Malachi 3:10, in the New King James Version. It reads as follows:

MALACHI 3

10 *'Bring all the tithes into the storehouse, that there may be food in My house, And try Me in this,' says the Lord of hosts, 'If I will not open for you the windows of heaven, And pour out for you such blessing, That* <u>there will</u> *not* <u>be room</u> *enough* <u>to receive it</u>,*' (NKJV)*

When we look at this verse, we notice that there are some words underscored. They are underscored, because these words were not in the original Hebrew text. When this passage was translated into English, the translators, to try to make sense out of the passage, added these underscored words. It is our personal opinion that these underscored words have actually distorted the meaning of the passage. If we simply read the passage without these underscored words, it would say, **"and open for you the windows of heaven, pour out for you blessing. That not enough."** I (Earl) believe that the author meant, "That is not enough." What is not enough? I believe that he is saying that the tithe coming into the local storehouse is not enough. Remember, he said in verse 9 that Israel had robbed God in not only tithes, but also in offerings or giving. I believe that the tithe is similar to the minimum balance in a bank account. It is the minimum balance necessary to keep active the "Treasures in Heaven" account. In chapter four, we have talked extensively about the "Treasures in Heaven" account. However, tithing, in and of itself, is not enough, as abundance flows through an open window. The tithe merely opens the windows of heaven.

While the tithe keeps the heavenly account active, offerings are that which release abundant blessing for the other three uses of money besides the tithe and provision. It is offerings, or giving that multiply in the account to pour out through that open window of heaven for financial blessing to meet the budget beyond basic need and to provide overflow.

I (Craig) believe that it is important for us as believers to separate in our minds and accounts the tithe from offerings. The tithe is simply a fiduciary account belonging to the Lord, which we manage on His behalf. It keeps the "Treasures in Heaven" account active and open. But it is not enough. Offerings release blessing and are used for entirely different purposes than the tithe.

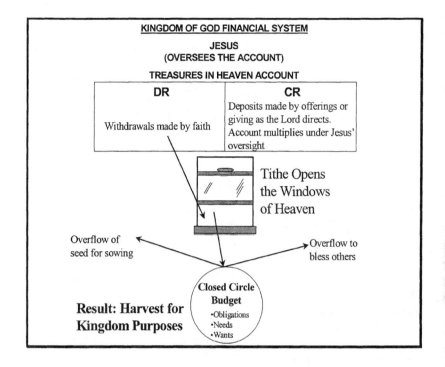

A physical example that I (Earl) use to help our understanding is to picture the function of an Automatic Teller machine (ATM) card. When you put the card in the machine, a physical window opens on many machines (or at least it will activate a "Windows" operating system!), so you can complete your transactions. In this example, your ATM card is like the tithe. However, there is no release of activity until your password activates your account. This operation is like your offerings or giving. In order for Kingdom finances to function, it requires tithe and offerings. This method is God's Ancient Path to keep us free from falling under the curse of the world system, where we are consigned to its limitations and failures!

Another purpose of the tithe is to deliver an individual or family from financial fear. As God's love is experienced in His faithfulness to provide, His perfect love casts out fear (1 John 4:18). If a family never places themselves in a position of needing God's supernatural power, then the spirit of Mammon will continue to govern them through fear.

If you have never established tithing as a regular habit in your life, and you're just considering that now, it may scare you. This again is an indicator that Sparrow Faith is not yet established in your heart. The bottom line issue is, "Does my Father really love me?" I've found that life experience for many has proven to them that they haven't been provided for. This repeated life experience of not being provided for becomes a very strong internal image. This is what the Bible calls a "stronghold" in the mind (2 Corinthians 10:4-6). Past life experience tells us, "These principles will work for other people, but they don't work in my life. I've done this. I've tried these principles. I just can't get a hold of it"

No! The fact is that the word of God is true, and past life experience is not the determiner of your future. Life experience creates a stronghold, which begets more life experience. Have you noticed that the reality of life is actually birthed right out of the image in your heart? So, once an image in the heart is established, reality of life is going to flow right out of that image. Reality, then will confirm the original image. This cycle goes round and round and round. Image begets reality. Reality then confirms the image, which becomes stronger and begets more reality, which confirms image, which becomes stronger, and round and round and round you go. So then, initiating the practice of tithing goes against everything within us screaming out that we will perish. If God's supernatural power does not likewise initiate, we will perish. However, God is faithful, and this is His mechanism of banishing fear from out hearts and establishing Sparrow Faith toward Him.

Let me (Craig) share with you a powerful testimony of how even the intent to tithe releases God's supernatural power. After attending a three-day seminar covering these principles, a woman wrote me the following letter.

> "I wanted to write you this letter to thank you for bringing the financial seminar to our family and to me. I wasn't planning on doing the seminar. I felt I had a fairly good grip on our financial situation and we were doing okay considering our situation.
>
> After Sunday night my whole world was blown apart. I realized that **I did have a good grip on my finances** and God only came into the picture when things got tough and we needed help. As a couple we could

tick off every single symptom of the spirit of Mammon. The ones I didn't tick, my husband did.

When you started to talk about the tithe I panicked. There was no way we could afford to tithe 10% of our gross income and stay in the black. It is not as if we can make any savings by living more frugally! To tithe for us would mean that we would need to seek God's provision for the shortfall each week. To me that meant losing my control and struggling from week to week just to get by.

Up until last night God's provision to me meant just enough to get by, with heaps of faith and always at the last minute. I spent the whole of yesterday trying to come to a place of feeling comfortable with tithing. The thing that made it really hard was that we both believed God had given us His blessing to increase our mortgage so we could build a garage and begin to fit back into our house. This had become something we desperately needed with our 3rd child due in three months (or so I thought).

Through all this turmoil, I know we had to start tithing no matter what, and that God really did want me to see Him as my provider. I know that letting go of the controlling fear I have had in this area of my life is a huge key for me in giving God my heart. By the end of the day yesterday I felt relatively at peace with going ahead with the tithe and letting go of the garage if that needed to happen. I felt ready to start seeing God as my provider for the first time ever.

All I can say now is God is incredible. I could not go last night as I had a class of my own to teach. My husband came home and said "you're not going to believe this!" (A very unexpected and supernatural source had just opened for them releasing a significant lump sum amount of money to them.) God has just blessed us with all this money. It was like He was saying, "Here, look! This is how I can provide when you let Me."

Today I am so excited, not because we now have all this money, and we can start to look towards a garage, but because I started to catch onto God's principles of finance. I can feel in my heart that my attitudes are changing. From living in a mentality of "I can't afford it;" I am starting to feel in my heart that if I let go and let God anything is possible. For the first time in my life I know that God does want prosperity for us. At the same time I am also seeing that the prosperity is not just for us, but so that He can use us to help others.

I thank you and thank God for the revelation that I have had over the last two days. It is like the blindfolds have come off and I am starting to see things clearly for the first time.

God bless you,
Nicky Smith, Upper Hutt, New Zealand

Another powerful purpose in tithing is that it breaks the power of the spirit of Mammon and profanes the sacred properties that we are tempted to ascribe to money. Money was designed by man for buying and selling, for receiving something of equal exchange. When we give money with no expectation of receiving something of equal value, we are introducing money to grace. Mammon tries to tell us that when we give, we now have diminished purchasing power. However, we are proclaiming to the spirit of Mammon, that money has no power in our lives, and that because God is our source, power to have our needs met, or fulfill our vision is not diminished one iota.

Although neither God nor the church needs our money, God does use the tithe as a primary channel, through which to fund Kingdom work in His church. The Lord could cause Kingdom work to be done without the tithe, but it is the usual method He employs for funding Kingdom expansion.

TITHING VS. TITHER

HOW: Since God is not after money, but rather after the heart, the attitude with which we tithe is very critical. God wants us to be tithers who bring the tithe to the storehouse. Many people are tithing but never become tithers. What is the difference between someone who tithes and a tither? The difference has to do with the attitude and active involvement. I (Earl) do a lot of flying, but I am not a flyer! If I were a flyer, then I could sit up on the flight deck and pilot the plane. However, since I am not a flyer, I take no active part in the flight of the airplanes on which I ride. Now what does it take to become a tither?

GENESIS 4

3   *And in the course of time Cain brought to the Lord an offering of the fruit of the ground.*

4   *And Abel brought of the first-born of the flock and the fat portions. And the Lord had respect and regard for Abel and for his offering.*

5 But for Cain and his offering He had no respect or regard. So Cain was exceedingly angry and indignant, and looked sad and depressed.

6 And the Lord said to Cain, Why are you angry? And why do you look sad and dejected?

7 If you do well, will you not be accepted? And if you do not do well, sin crouches at the door; its desire is for you, and you must master it. (Amplified)

In this passage, we will see that Abel was a tither, but Cain merely tithed. Some people have tried to make the case that the reason Abel's sacrifice was accepted, and Cain's was not, was that Abel brought an offering of animals, whose blood could be shed, while Cain merely brought some of the harvest of his fields. However, we believe that the primary difference had to do with the attitudes of these two men, not the substance of the offerings.

Notice the expression in verse three, "in the course of time," or some translations say "end of days," which is a Hebrew idiom expressing a time of tithing. We notice the different responses of these two men when it came to tithe. Abel was overjoyed as he brought the tithe of the firstborn and the fat portions. The fat portions, the extra layers of fat that some of the animals develop on the upper portion of the thigh. This fat can act as a insulator from the cold ground at certain times of the year. The extra fat made this area a choice piece of meat for eating. Abel's attitude was to bring over and above what was required. He wanted to give and bless, and God accepted Abel's tithe.

Cain's response, on the other hand, was totally different. When God had not respect or regard for his tithe, he was exceedingly angry and fell into self-pity. What was happening in his life? God asked him why he was so angry. Of course, God knew what was going on in Cain's life, but He asked the question to see if Cain was in touch with his own feelings. In verse seven, God explains the situation and shows Cain the way out. He told him, "If you 'do well,' will you not be accepted?" This phrase "to do well" again is a Hebrew expression, which means "to adjust one's attitude." So the verse would better be translated, "if you adjust your attitude, will you not be accepted? And if you do not adjust your attitude, sin crouches at the door; its desire is for you, and you must master it."

What a relevant statement for us today! Our attitude determines our future. How we respond to the people and circumstances of our lives today either qualifies or disqualifies us for what God had in mind for us tomorrow. Here in Genesis, chapter four, God is speaking about attitude when it comes to tithing. I (Earl) have found over the years that Bible teaching about tithing brings out various responses in people. Some get mad. Some get sad. And some get glad! The point is that our attitude, which is reflected both internally and externally determines whether we are true tithers or just ones who are tithing. This point is further highlighted when we look at Hebrews, chapter eleven.

HEBREWS 11

4 *[Prompted, actuated] by faith Abel brought God a better and more acceptable sacrifice than Cain, because of which it was testified of him that he was righteous— [that is,] that he was upright and in right standing with God— and God bore witness by accepting and acknowledging his gifts. And although he died, yet through [the incident] he is still speaking. (Amplified)*

In the last part of this verse, we find it is relevant for today— 'he is still speaking.' As we bring our tithe, an attitude check on our part is required in order for the tithe to accomplish what God intents for it to do— namely open up the windows of heaven under your Treasures in Heaven account.

HOLY UNTO THE LORD

Another critical aspect of tithing has to do with our attitude toward the tithe, itself. In the following scripture, God answered for Israel two critical questions regarding the tithe. We would do well to answer these same two questions in our own lives regarding the tithe.

The two questions are: To whom does the tithe belong? Secondly, what type of money is the tithe?

LEVITICUS 27

30 And all the tithe of the land, whether of the seed of the land or of the fruit of the tree, is the Lord's. It is holy to the Lord. (NKJV)

In answer to these two questions above, we see the following answers. Firstly, the tithe is the Lord's. It does not belong to you. It belongs to the Lord. This means that you are merely a fiduciary steward or manager on behalf of the Lord of that which belongs to Him. Secondly, the tithe is holy. When I (Craig) first saw this scripture it shocked me. I had always considered that the tithe involved my giving 10% of my money to the Lord. It was a major paradigm shift for me to realize that I was not giving my money to the Lord, but rather I was managing His money and returning that to Him.

What does it mean for something or someone to be holy? I believe that we tend to have a very distorted view of the word "holy." Many people think that this word connotes a particular standard of behavior or something pertaining only to God. Actually, the word simply means, "dedicated, or set aside." The word "holy" is meaningless without an object. If something is holy (dedicated), the obvious question to be answered is, "dedicated to what, or whom?" There is only One in the universe to Whom holiness applies without an object, and that is the Lord. He is holy unto Himself. Everything and everyone else must be holy (dedicated) unto something, or someone.

In order to more clearly understand this concept, let me give you an example. Suppose that there are five telephone lines coming into an office. Four of them are commonly used for communication, but one line is dedicated to the fax machine. We could rightly say, that the fifth line is holy unto the fax machine. This is the meaning of the word. We cannot say that a man is holy. We must know unto what or whom. If he is holy unto his wife, this means that he is dedicated to her such that he does not have the same relationship with anyone else. He shares certain parts of his life uniquely with her and pursues certain activities only with her.

The opposite of holy is common. The other four lines in the office are common lines to be used for anything, but the fifth line is holy unto the fax machine. When something is dedicated as holy, it must be kept separate from that which is common.

Thus, with this understanding, we can better understand what it means for a Christian to be holy unto the Lord. It means he/she is dedicated or set aside for relationship with the Lord. His/her behavior and activities may be voluntarily limited compared to those who are not dedicated unto the Lord simply because of that choice to belong to the Lord.

Now regarding finances, what does it mean to be holy? Let's look at this example. Suppose you sign a contract to purchase a house and place a down payment of $5,000 on the house. The deal is expected to close in two months. Where is your $5,000 placed, and how is it used? Normally, it is placed in an escrow or trust account and is managed by an escrow or trust agent. We could say that this money is holy unto your house closing.

What would happen if the trust agent in the next month were personally a little short of funds to pay his bills? So, knowing that the money would not be needed for closing for another six weeks, he personally "borrows" $2,000 from the trust account with the intent of repaying it before closing. Even if he does indeed replace this money before closing, if this is discovered, what will be done with this trust agent in most countries? He will be tried and placed in jail. Why? Because he has violated a fiduciary responsibility to manage that trust account on your behalf. Or to put it very simply, **he has touched holy money for himself.**

Suppose instead that the trust agent does not even deposit your $5,000 in a trust account, but rather just commingles the funds with that of his own personal account. He intends to supply these funds at closing, but they remain in his account for the two months. Or suppose a stock (share) broker commingles the deposited funds of his clients with that of his own personal account. Even if he has the intent to provide the funds to his clients upon their demand, if this is discovered, he will go to jail. In both these cases, this money is holy.

What, then, does the Bible mean when it tells us that the tithe is holy unto the Lord? I believe that we must understand this in the same way we understand an escrow or trust account. Firstly, the money, which represents the tithe, does not belong to you. It belongs to the Lord, and you are a fiduciary agent charged with the duty of receiving and delivering it to the "storehouse."

Since most Christians do not understand the concept of holiness to start with, they do not treat the tithe as holy. Many do not recognize that the tithe is the Lord's but rather think that it is theirs, and they feel very magnanimous in giving it. I believe that to treat the tithe as holy means that we firstly recognize that it is the Lord's, not mine. Secondly, I do not commingle the Lord's tithe with other funds available to me that are "common." I must treat the tithe as a trust account managed on behalf of the Lord.

As soon as my (Craig's) two sons were old enough to have any money, I began to teach them about the tithe. I did so by giving them each four separate jars. Ten cents of every dollar went directly into the tithe jar. Other percentages were then designated for offerings, saving, and spending. In this way, my sons learned that the tithe is holy and is never commingled with other common funds.

When my wife and I (Craig) were first married, we opened a joint checking account, and a separate tithe account. Whenever we received any salary or other money, we immediately wrote a check for 10% and deposited it in our tithe account. This money was then kept separate from the money we used for our household living expenses. We managed the tithe account as a trust account for the Lord. Thus, when we gave it to the storehouse, we never felt any financial pressure because we never included that money in our accounting of money available for household expenses or for any other purpose. We never saw it in our own checking account.

In recent years we have kept the money together in the same physical bank account, but have segregated our tithe money in a separate computer account with our financial software program. Thus, again, we do not see the Lord's tithe money in our personal account. We keep it as a trust account holy unto the Lord.

I suggest that you find a way to make the Lord's tithe, over which He has made you a manager, holy unto Him. If you have struggled with your management of the Lord's tithe, I suggest that you open a separate bank account or that you get cash envelopes or jars. Separate the tithe from the rest of your common money and keep the tithe holy unto the Lord.

We believe that this management of the tithe is the very first level of fiduciary management into which you can enter. If you are not even faithful in the entry level management of the Lord's tithe, why would you expect that the Lord would entrust you with any greater management of His resources? I have met several Christians who would like to manage much financial resource, which they claim they would like to channel into the Kingdom of God. However, they are not even faithful in the entry-level management of the Lord's tithe.

CHEREM: DEDICATED TO GOD

LEVITICUS 27

28 *But no thing that a man shall devote to the Lord of all that he has, whether of man or beast or of the field of his possession, shall be sold or redeemed; every devoted thing is holy to the Lord. (Amplified)*

The Hebrew word used in this verse translated "devoted" is the word "cherem." The biblical word cherem literally means in Hebrew, "dedicated to God," thus making it unavailable for your use. Thus, anything that is considered cherem is dedicated to the Lord and, therefore, is holy unto the Lord.

LEVITICUS 27

30 And all the tithe of the land, whether of the seed of the land or of the fruit of the tree, it is the Lord's; it is holy to the Lord. (Amplified)

We talked earlier about the fact that the tithe is holy or dedicated. If you don't deal with it properly by bringing it to the storehouse, it will be consumed, and unavailable to you. So the tithe could also be seen as similar to that which is cherem, or dedicated to destruction. Even if you try to keep it, it will not be available for your use, because it is already dedicated to another.

Many times, its owner dedicates that which is cherem to destruction. An example of something dedicated to destruction is a bar of radioactive plutonium. It is continually decaying, and this decay cannot be stopped. If you bury it in your house or carry it in your pocket, its decaying nature will begin to destroy you as well. Plutonium, thus, can be likened to the biblical concept of cherem, that which is dedicated to destruction.

Let's look at a biblical example involving this concept of cherem. In ancient Israel, it was common practice for soldiers to be paid with the spoil from the cities they had conquered. They were not paid a wage by their government as in modern times. When an army captured a city, the soldiers got to keep all the gold, silver and livestock and got to take the captured people as their slaves. This was their pay for risking their lives to conquer the city.

However, when Israel crossed over the Jordan River and went in to conquer the land of Cannan, certain cities were designated by God to be "Cherem" cities. Now, what is a Cherem city? A Cherem city is a one that is devoted to total destruction. This means, that in such a dedicated city, as a soldier, you must touch nothing. You don't take the gold. You don't take the silver. You take no prisoners or slaves. The gold and silver all go into the treasury of the Lord, and you burn the entire city. It is entirely devoted to destruction. You don't touch any of it. So, as a soldier, you know that such a city is conquered for the Lord without pay. The soldier must risk his life to conquer the city, but without any hope of personal gain. When conquering other non-cherem cities, the soldiers were able to take slaves, and keep whatever valuables they could find.

In Joshua chapter six, we read that the very first city to be conquered in Canaan, Jericho was designated by God as a Cherem city, dedicated to destruction. The Israeli soldiers were to utterly destroy the city and place all of the valuables in the treasury of the Lord.

JOSHUA 6

17 *And the city and all that is in it shall be* (Cherem) *devoted to the Lord (for destruction); only Rahab the harlot and all who are with her in her house shall live because she hid the messengers whom we sent.*

18 *But you, keep yourselves from the* (Cherem) *accursed and devoted thing, lest when you have devoted it (to destruction), you take of the* (Cherem) *accursed thing, and so make the camp of Israel accursed, and trouble it. (Amplified)*

Now this word "cherem" is translated in English as "accursed," "under the ban," "devoted," or "dedicated to destruction." So, the Lord told Israel that by all means, they were to abstain from the cherem in Jericho. Joshua conveyed this instruction to Israel. However, there was one soldier who did not believe that this instruction applied to him. Apparently, Achan believed that this was just some, arbitrary edict from God that had no real purpose or practical consequence. Achan, therefore, decided to take some of the valuables he found in Jericho and hide them under the floor of his tent, unbeknownst to anyone.

The consequence of Achan's taking and hiding cherem from Jericho was that Israel lost a very simple battle at Ai. This action of Achan did not affect just Achan, but rather affected the entire nation of Israel. After this battle was lost, Joshua, as a wise leader, sought the Lord as the reason for the defeat. He was not looking just in the natural realm, but he realized that there was something affecting the battle in the spirit realm. We read of his interaction with the Lord in the following passage.

JOSHUA 7

10 The Lord said to Joshua, "Get up! Why do you lie upon your face?

11 Israel has sinned; they have transgressed My covenant which I commanded them. They have taken some of the things devoted [for destruction] (Cherem); they have stolen, and lied, and put them among their own baggage.

12 That is why the Israelites could not stand before their enemies, but fled before them; they are accursed and have become devoted [for destruction]. I will cease to be with you unless you destroy the accursed [devoted] things among you.

13 Up, sanctify (set apart for a holy purpose) the people, and say, 'Sanctify yourselves for tomorrow; for thus says the Lord, the God of Israel, 'There is an accursed thing in the midst of you, O Israel.' You cannot stand before your enemies until you take way from among you the thing devoted [to destruction].'" (Amplified)

The important principle that is seen in this passage is that the people of Israel could not stand before their enemies as long as someone in their midst had considered that which was holy, devoted to destruction, as common and had buried it amongst his own possessions. Many people have done exactly this with their tithe, not recognizing that it is similar to the Hebrew concept of cherem, holy unto the Lord. It is not common, but rather is dedicated money.

Secondly, we need to recognize that when we take the tithe, which is holy like cherem, and bury it amongst our own possessions, we not only affect ourselves, but also others in our own congregation. We have observed that in a congregation in which the tithe is considered holy, and the majority of people in the congregation are tithers, there tends to be an open heaven over this congregation. There is more of a strong sense of God's presence in their services, many miracles, healings, supernatural words, etc. In this congregation, businesses prosper, houses sell, people are employed, and the overall congregation tends to prosper.

On the contrary, we have observed that in a congregation where the tithe is not considered holy, and many people in the congregation are not tithers, the windows of heaven just seem to be closed over this congregation. Houses remain on the market unsold for months and years; people have difficulty receiving employment; businesses seem to be hindered, and the presence of God and His supernatural power do not seem to be very evident. Everyone is affected when some touch the cherem. Many congregations will not be able to stand before their enemies until they help their people to understand that they must remove from their own possessions the cherem that they have buried. People must be taught that the tithe is cherem; that even if you try to keep it, because it is devoted to destruction, it will never be useable to you. They must be taught that the tithe is the Lord's, and it is holy unto Him.

Returning to a point we made earlier, we saw in Malachi 3:10 that the tithe opens the windows of heaven. From this, it is very easy to see why a church in which many people are not tithers frequently experiences a closed heaven over their congregation, while a church full of tithers experiences an open heaven. The Lord told us in Malachi that this would be the case.

ISRAEL'S USE OF THE TITHE

Let's now look at Deuteronomy 26, to see what the tithe was to be used for in Israel. There is in this scripture a pattern established for usage of the tithe, which we have observed is not common practice among most churches in our day.

DEUTERONOMY 26

13 *Then you shall say before the Lord your God, I have brought the hallowed thing (the tithe) out of my house, and moreover have given them to the <u>Levite, to the stranger and the sojourner, to the fatherless, and to the widow</u>, according to all your commandments which you have commanded me; I have not transgressed any of your commandments, neither have I forgotten them. (Amplified)*

For what purpose did Israel use the tithe? They used it for Levites, strangers, sojourners, fatherless and widows. Furthermore, we find other types of people in Nehemiah 10:38, 39. The tithe went to the priests, gatekeepers, and the singers. Isn't that interesting? The scriptural pattern established in Israel saw the tithe used for people, not for structures.

Now, how did Israel finance structures for God's purposes? They used offerings for this purpose. God instructed Israel to make a clear distinction between the tithe, which was used to support people, and offerings, which could be used for structures. Now, what is the common practice in our day? We usually mix the tithe and offering, making no distinction in its collection or in its usage. When pastors and church leaders make no distinction between tithe and offering, is it any wonder that church members do the same? Commonly, in a church service, a leader will say something such as, "Now we're going to receive our tithes and offerings." The concepts are mixed. The tithe is not made to be holy, neither in the minds of the church leaders, nor in the minds of the church members.

Imagine what would have happened if David had gone to the Levites and announced to them that God had instructed him to build a temple, and as a result of that, their support from the tithe would be diminished or eliminated for the next few years until the temple was completed. Of course, David did not do this. The tithe continued to go to the priest, Levite, widow, orphan, and stranger, even while the temple was being constructed. It was definitely not commingled with the offerings for the temple, as it was considered holy both by the leaders and the people. The tithe was used for a specific purpose and was not commingled in a general budget with offerings. I believe that this common practice of not considering the tithe holy unto the Lord by commingling the purpose and the actual funds of the tithe and offerings is offensive to the Lord. When there is no distinction made between the tithe and offerings by church leadership, there certainly will not be by any distinction made by the people.

SCRIPTURAL ATTITUDE CHECK

In an earlier part of this section, we saw that the primary distinction between one who tithes (Cain) and a tither (Abel) is the attitude and handling of the tithe. Thus, it is important for us to periodically check our own attitude regarding the Lord's tithe. We certainly want the tithe to accomplish God's purposes in our lives, namely to generate Sparrow Faith in our hearts, and to open the windows of heaven under our Treasures in Heaven account.

Principles for the preparation of our tithe, along with an attitude check, are found in Deuteronomy 26. This portion of scripture is dealing with the law concerning tithing and specifically the tithe that was given every third year. We believe that we can glean some principles that are highly relevant for us today from these scriptures.

DEUTERONOMY 26

1   *When you come into the land which the Lord your God gives you for an inheritance, and possess it, and live in it,*

2   *You shall take some of all the produce of the soil which you harvest from the land that the Lord your God gives you, and put it in a basket, and go to the place [the sanctuary] which the Lord your God has chosen as the abiding place for His name [and His presence].*

3   *And you shall go to the priest who is in office in those days, and say to him, I give thanks this day that I have come to the land which the Lord swore to our fathers to give us;*

4   *And the priest shall take the basket from your hand, and set it down before the alter of the Lord your God. (Amplified)*

The tithe was always on the medium of exchange that was used by people. The barter system used by farmers in that culture meant the tithe was in some form of product or produce. If you were an animal farmer, you brought one in ten of the increase of your flock or herd. A produce farmer would bring the 10% of the crop.

The first attitude check found in verse 3 is one of **thanksgiving**. Verses 5 through 9 recount the journey of the children of Israel from

Egypt to "a land flowing with milk and honey." This was to be a time of remembering of how God had brought them out of bondage into His provision. For us, as we prepare our tithe, it is good to recount what God has done in our lives, how we have been delivered from darkness into His marvelous light, from death to Life Eternal. This preparation of heart positions us in attitude.

DEUTERONMY 26

10 *And now, behold, I bring the first fruits of the ground, which You, O Lord have given me. And you shall set it down before the Lord your God, and worship before the Lord your God;*

11 *And you shall rejoice in all the good which the Lord your God has given you and your household, you and the Levite, and the stranger and the sojourner among you. (Amplified)*

The next two principles are found in verses 10 and 11, namely **worship and rejoicing**. The Lord has restored to His Body the significance of praise and worship. I (Earl) can look back thirty years and see the release in worship ministries that God has and is restoring to His Church. Many churches incorporate the receiving of the tithe and offerings (giving) during the worship time. Bringing our tithe is an act of worship.

Rejoicing is an attitude of heart that accompanies a tither. When I (Earl) was growing up in the 1950's, my parents took me to church every Sunday. I can recall the time when the pastor would announce that it was time to receive the tithes and offerings. There was an immediate hush over the audience. The organist would start to play, as I recall, a type of dirge. The ushers would come down the aisles without a smile and perfunctorily pass the plates down the rows. People looked sad. Some would look straight ahead and, without a smile, put the envelope in the plate and pass it on. I always thought, "This is a sad time. It will be nice when this is over!" It seemed that the church then lightened up again, and we went on with the service.

It was many years later that I was in a church in Hawaii, and during the worship time, the pastor announced that is was time for the receiving of tithes and offerings. Some young people at the rear of the auditorium jumped up and spoke out, "Yes, Yes! Praise God!" The ushers came down the aisles and stood at the front, with big smiles on their faces. The worship band broke out into an up-tempo selection. Then people stood and shouted to the Lord with a loud voice. Row by row, they came to the front and placed their tithes and their offerings in the plates held by the ushers. After circulating around the church, they returned to their places, and the worship continued. This experience shattered forever my stereotype of how the receiving of tithes and the giving of offerings should be done! I can picture the children of Israel bringing their first fruits to the tabernacle, with dancing and great joy!

DEUTERONOMY 26

13 *Then you shall say before the Lord your God, I have brought the hallowed things out of my house, and moreover have given them to the Levite, to the stranger and the sojourner, to the fatherless, and the widow, according to all you have commanded me; I have not transgressed any of your commandments, neither have I forgotten them.*

14 *I have not eaten of the tithe in my mourning [making the tithe unclean], nor have I handled any of it when I was unclean, or given any of it to the dead; I have hearkened to the voice of the Lord my God, and have done according to all that You have commanded. (Amplified)*

The next principle in the preparation of the tithe is to review our past obedience to the Lord. Notice in the latter part of verse 13, they made a confession that they had been obedient, for **they had not transgressed any of God's commandments,** nor had they forgotten them. Have we been obedient to what God has said in His Word? If there has been any violation, then there is call to repentance over these issues. In verse 14, they proclaimed that **they had not eaten of the tithe**. Many people eat their tithe by using it for their bills or for other uses. I hear statements like "If I tithed, I would not be able to pay the rent!" Of course, such people have not understood yet Who is their source, and have not realized to Whom the tithe belongs, and what kind of money it is.

The late Malcolm McGregor wrote a book entitled, "Your Money Matters." In the book he made the following offer. "If after three months of tithing, you are unable to pay your bills, send them to me... ."[6] He frequently reported that in 14 years of making this offer, no one to that point had ever taken him up on the offer. God honors His Word, because the tithe belongs to the Lord, as we have seen, and it positions us in Sparrow Faith to be able to receive God's provision.

The next point in the spiritual checkup states, "**nor have I handled any of it when I was unclean**." There were specific things in the Law that made people unclean. When in this condition, they were not to handle the tithe. Since the ceremonial law has been fulfilled in Jesus, the externals now are conditions of the heart. Jesus said that it was not what entered into a man that defiled him, but rather what proceeded out of the mouth from the heart that brings defilement (Matthew 15:18-20). One of the things that Jesus taught about when bringing offerings deals with unforgiveness. Thus, part of the spiritual checkup is to ask the Spirit of God to search our hearts for any area of unforgiveness and repent of it.

Next is the statement, "**or given it to the dead**." There was a practice in Israel, in which money or bartered goods were placed with a dead body at its burial. The law stated that the tithe was not to be used for that purpose. The tithe is given to the One who lives. Jesus is to be the recipient of His tithe. This was established with Abram and Melchizedek in Genesis 14:17-21. Jesus refers to Himself as being after the order of Melchizedek in Hebrews 6:20. We do not know where Melchizedek came from. Some scholars think that he was a preincarnation of Jesus in the earth. The point is that tithing is our living response to Jesus that establishes His Lordship in our financial arena.

---

[6] Malcolm MacGregor with Stanley G. Baldwin, *Your Money Matters*, Bethany Fellowship Inc., Updated 1980, Minneapolis MN, p. 53

Finally, there is the statement in verse 14, "**I have harkened to the voice of the Lord my God and have done according to all that You have commanded me**." Have we listened to His voice and been obedient to the promptings of the Holy Spirit? This spiritual checkup is tied to tithing. It has been said that if we tithe correctly, it will keep us right with God! What a thought! Preparing that which God calls "holy" correctly will be a vehicle to check our attitudes and obedient responses to God on a weekly basis, as we bring our tithe to the storehouse.

DEUTERONOMY 26

15 Look down from Your holy habitations, from Heaven, and bless Your people Israel, and the land which You have given us, as You swore to our fathers, a land flowing with milk and honey. (Amplified)

We see in this verse the concept of an open heaven about which Malachi wrote when he described the opening up the windows of heaven (Malachi 3:10) and a blessing being poured out when the tithe was brought into the storehouse.

Let's now review these attitudes regarding the tithe listed in Deuteronomy 26.

1. Thanksgiving and remembering what God has done for us
2. Worship
3. Rejoicing
4. Obedience to God's Word
5. Not to be used to meet your needs
6. Deal with unforgiveness— having clean hands.
7. Be reminded of Jesus' Lordship over your finances
8. Obedience to the promptings of the Holy Spirit

Blessing on your family and an open heaven is the result.

CHAPTER 5
BREAD FOR EATING

JOHN 4:23-24

SPIRIT	TRUTH
Faith *Romans 10:17* Word	Faith *Luke 17:5-10* Obedience
GRACE	**BUILDING BLOCKS**
2 CORINTHIANS 9:8	1. RECOGNIZE AND RENOUNCE THE SPIRIT OF MAMMON
And God is able to make all grace (every favor and earthly blessing) come to you in abundance, so that you may always and under all circumstances and whatever the need, be self sufficient, possessing enough to require no aid or support and furnished in abundance for every good work and charitable donation. (Amplified)	(Heart allegiance goes to God alone)
	2. ESTABLISH SPARROW FAITH
	(God is my source)
	3. ESTABLISH THE TITHE
	(Be a tither rather than just tithing)
	4. BECOME GOD'S MANAGER
	(Become accountable to God for administration of present resources)

The second use of money described in 2 Corinthians 9 is what is termed "bread for eating," or "bread for your food" in the King James Version. This deals with money that we spend for personal consumption, the things we buy. Many Christians have not included God in this area of their lives. However, God is very interested in how we personally use money. The Mammon spirit drives our consumer-oriented society by creating a great sense of "need." The growth of an industrial society is tied to production of goods and services for the meeting of needs. As we in the western world moved into the 1900's, we discovered new ways to create needs that were not formerly perceived. We told people that there were things they did not know existed and they should want them. Now we have moved into the creation of a "wants" category. If this trend is coupled with our "have to have it now" generation, and our inability to say "No," we have a lethal situation that is bringing many people into bondage to debt in order to follow the Mammon piper.

After establishing the tithe in our lives, the next step is to become a manager/steward of God's resources. As stewards of money before the Lord, we are to make money our slave, rather than being a slave to money. In so doing, we must now come to the place where we personally answer the question **"How Much Is Enough?"** This is not a flashback to the 60's, where there was a backlash among baby-boomers over their parents' consumerism, but rather a genuine call to hear God's heart on the issue and the instruction of His Word. To answer the question posed is not to invoke some arbitrary set of rules to try to curb consumption. No one can answer the question for you. You must be able to look the Lord in the eyes and honestly answer the question. Jesus knows what is correct for you and He has an opinion on everything pertaining to your finances. I (Earl) have found that directly addressing this area of personal consumption is the last taboo in our society and in the church. No one talks about it, unless someone gets in trouble and files bankruptcy. At this point, it is usually nothing more than gossip. Our schools educate in all other fields, but one rarely finds a course in Money 101? In church we teach on tithing, giving, sowing and reaping, and prosperity, but leave people to their own devices and perhaps vices regarding the management of their own personal consumption. Most people are then highly influenced by the spirit of Mammon and never really understand what is happening to them long-term.

God's heart is to bless us and provide financially for His calling and purposes to be fulfilled in our lives. However, if we have never answered in writing the question, "How much is enough," then any financial increase that the Lord brings to us is likely to simply be consumed without thought or plan. The problem in lack is not God's unwillingness to provide increase, but rather our unwillingness to manage, as a steward, that which is provided. The Lord is looking for those who are faithful stewards of their money used for personal consumption. These He could trust to manage huge releases of finances for His Kingdom purposes. In His parable in Luke 16, Jesus talks about a manager/steward who was called to account for his usage of his master's goods. Let's now look at this parable.

LUKE 16

1   *Also [Jesus] said to the disciples, "There was a certain rich man who had a manager of his estate, and accusations [against this man were brought] to him, that he was squandering his [master's] possessions.*

2   *And he called him and said to him, 'What is this I hear about you? Turn in the account of your management [of my affairs], for you can be [my] manager no longer.'*

3   *And the manager of the estate said to himself, 'What shall I do, seeing that my master is taking the management away from me? I am not able to dig, and I am ashamed to beg.*

4   *I have come to know what I will do, seeing that they [my master's debtors] may accept and welcome me into their houses when I am put out of the management'.*

5   *So he summoned his master's debtor one by one, and he said to the first, 'How much do you owe my master?'*

6   *He said, 'A hundred measures [about nine hundred gallons] of oil.' And he said to him, 'Take back your written acknowledgement of obligation and sit down quickly and write fifty [about four hundred and fifty gallons].'*

7   *After that he said to another, 'And how much do you owe?' He said, 'A hundred measures [about nine hundred bushels] of wheat.' He said to him, 'Take back your written acknowledgement of the obligation and write eighty [about seven hundred bushels].'*

8   *And [his] master praised the dishonest (unjust) manager for acting shrewdly and prudently; for the sons of this age are*

shrewder and more prudent and wiser in [relation to] their own generation— that is, to their own age and kind— than are the sons of light." (Amplified)

To prepare ourselves to understand the parable, we need to note that Jesus is talking to His disciples and teaching them. In verse 14, we see a group of Pharisees who are listening to all that Jesus is saying, and it is also affecting them. They began to sneer, ridicule and scoff at Him! Obviously, Jesus is using the parable to point out something in the actions of the Pharisees that was wrong.

The manager or steward of the rich master had gotten himself into some type of mismanagement of the master's affairs. There is a call for accountability, as should be the case, in the life of every steward. It appears that the steward knows when the accountability review takes place, that he will lose his job. He now moves into one element of the management function, known as planning. He is concerned about his future and uses his mind to create a plan to solve the problem. He assesses the situation and comments that he has a back problem and cannot dig. His pride rises and tells him that it would be a shame to beg. His mind devises a plan. Proverbs 16:9 states that a man's mind plans his way, but the Lord directs his steps and makes them sure. That is how the Lord expects us to function. However, in the life of the steward, since he has no relationship with the Lord, he simply uses his natural mind and the world system to solve his problem.

His plan involves the master's debtors. In verses 6 and 7, the steward reduces the debt owed the master by 50% and 20% respectively. Now if you were one of the master's debtors, how would you feel about this transaction? How would you feel about your relationship with the steward? Probably, you would be thankful and willing to help the steward in any possible way. The steward used the reduction of what was owed by the debtors to buy favor for himself.

The master was aware of what the steward had done, because he praised him for acting shrewdly and prudently (verse 8). Why would he praise the steward? This seems to make no sense. If I, as a business owner, had been stolen from by my manager, who, without authorization, reduced my creditors' debts, I would be the last one to praise the steward. There must be something more than meets the eye taking place in this parable.

Donald Kraybill in his insightful book, *The Upside-Down Kingdom*,[7] sheds light on this parable, which explains this seeming paradox of the master's reaction to the steward's cunning. Kraybill explains the following cultural setting in place in Israel at the time Jesus told this parable. The Pharisees, we are told, were lovers of money (verse 14). The Law of Moses posed a significant hindrance to the Pharisees, as it precluded charging interest of fellow Jews or strangers who lived in the land. The Law placed restrictions in the area of financial activity. This is a problem if you are a lover of money. The Pharisees, being themselves the interpreters of the Law, looked for loopholes, and even created some for themselves.

One significant loophole used at the time, was a crafted by the Pharisees, called the Law of Immediate Necessity. Now, this law worked in the following manner. If someone borrowed money for the purpose of meeting an immediate need, such as payroll, current operating expenses, etc. then when there was agreement to lend the money, no interest could be charged. However, if the borrower wanted the money for a purpose other than that of immediate necessity, such as purchasing inventory, then interest could be charged. The Law of Moses did not endorse this way of operating. It was rather a fabrication of the Pharisees designed to make money.

Thus, the stewards, who were managing inventory, would lend the master's inventory to debtors at interest. Usually this was done without the master's knowledge. (Thus, the first fractional-reserve banking system was born.) Since the Pharisees needed a method of implementing this law that would benefit them, they worked in conjunction with stewards who would charge interest to the debtors. The stewards collected the interest and cut the Pharisees in on a part of this profit. The steward then would be a front man for the Pharisees, who kept their cloak of religion as a cover for the Mammon-dominated lives they actually led. When the master was

---

[7] Donald B. Kraybill, *The Upside Down Kingdom*, Revised Edition 1990, Scottdale, PA Herald Pres, pp. 113-116

informed that the steward was involved in wasting the master's goods, the steward was called to account. In Jesus' parable, the steward, out of fear, called the master's debtors and returned to them the interest. In so doing, he was buying favor with the debtors for his future needs. The master praised the steward for doing what was right in returning the ill-gotten gain.

We can now see why the Pharisees scoffed at and derided Jesus when He told this parable. Jesus was teaching His disciples, but there happened to be present in the audience that day stewards, masters, and Pharisees. Can you imagine the embarrassment of the Pharisees as Jesus exposed this entire system of injustice to the masters in the crowd, who had no knowledge of this activity? The Pharisees were supposed to be the sons of light, and Jesus exposed them in front of the masters by telling this parable. They should have been protecting the common person through godly interpretation of the Law. Instead, they were interpreting the Law in such a way as to enrich themselves at the expense of the common person. These actions were directly contrary to the heart of God for people. These Pharisees who were supposed to be sons of light and should have been siding with humanity against the spirit of Mammon, were instead, enslaving people to that spirit. Jesus states that the sons of the age (in this case, the steward) acted more prudently than the sons of light (the Pharisees.) Jesus had exposed their operation, and they were furious.

In verse 8, we hear Jesus drawing a contrast between the sons of this age and the sons of light. The construction of the Greek text would imply that this contrast should not be that way. In other words, the sons of light need to be as shrewd and prudent and wise as the sons of this world. Who are the sons of light today? As Christians, we are the sons of light. Jesus said, "you are the light of the world" (Matthew 5:14). The steward was planning ahead, and the sons of light ought to do the same. Now the steward was manipulating with money to buy favor, which Jesus addressed next.

LUKE 16

9   And I tell you, make friends for yourselves by means of unrighteous Mammon [that is, deceitful riches, money possessions], so that when it fails, they [those you have favored] may receive and welcome you into the everlasting habitations (dwellings). (Amplified)

If one uses or manipulates with money to buy favor, all he will receive is what Mammon can provide. Those who submit to the use of money in this manner also come under the influence of the Mammon spirit. The Mammon spirit does not have everlasting habitations in heaven! This fact is a serious warning for us! As sons of light, God must be our source rather than our trusting in our employment, or investments. Sparrow Faith thus builds confidence in God and deals with the fear that the enemy would try to build into our lives through adverse circumstances.

One of the conclusions drawn from this parable is that we need to plan ahead for our financial situation. We have touched on verses 10-13 in Luke 16, previously where Jesus told us that faithfulness in properly using money is the qualification for true riches. If we use money to manipulate or enslave people, then we are in league with the spirit of Mammon and have disqualified ourselves from being a steward of God's resources. We are to use money for its legitimately designed purposes: buying and selling, and for giving and meeting needs.

LUKE 16

11   Therefore, if you have not been faithful in the [case of] the unrighteous Mammon— the deceitful riches, money, possessions— who will entrust to you the true riches? (Amplified)

The translators, to give the word "true" an object, have added the word "riches." We recognize that when unrighteous Mammon is controlling riches and money, it is trying to give it validity in the hearts of people to trust in riches and money as being a true source. In reality the unrighteous Mammon, which in this case is deceitful riches, is the false. God's heart is to entrust us with that which is true. The sobering truth in this verse is that our stewardship, faithful handling of riches and money is a condition for the release of that which God considers to be true.

LUKE 16

12 *And if you have not proved faithful in that which belongs to another [whether God or man], who will give you that which is your own [that is, the true riches]? (Amplified)*

God wants to give to us from His storehouse of truth. In scripture we find many of God's true attributes described as riches.

EPHESIANS 1

7 *In Him we have redemption (deliverance and salvation) through His blood, the remission (forgiveness) of our offenses (short comings and trespasses), in accordance with the riches and the generosity of His gracious favor,*

8 *Which He lavished upon us in every kind of wisdom and understanding (practical insight and prudence). (Amplified)*

God wants the riches of His grace (gracious favor) to be ours. Grace is a gift to us in Jesus, Who is full of grace and truth. However, it must be received through Him, as grace can be abused or rejected. If we learn to be faithful in that which belongs to another, simply managing riches and money correctly, we will steward the grace of God and the rest of God's true riches in like manner. God teaches us to be faithful and a good steward using tangible, physical things (riches and money), which belong to another (the world system) to prepare us to handle His intangible, but no less real "true riches."

There are other scripture references to true riches, such as the riches of Wisdom and Knowledge, Riches of His goodness, Riches of His Glory, and His unreachable riches. You may enjoy conducting a word study in your Bible concordance of the word "riches." You may then apply these meanings back to what God has available to us as a result of proper handling of money as spoken of in Luke 16:11. Let such a study reinforce and encourage you to develop the fruit of the Spirit of faithfulness, and the character quality of stewardship by practicing your stewardship on riches and money, so you can be released and entrusted with that which God considers true.

CHAPTER 6
CLOSE THE CIRCLE

JOHN 4:23-24

SPIRIT	TRUTH
Faith *Romans 10:17* Word **GRACE**	Faith *Luke 17:5-10* Obedience **BUILDING BLOCKS**
2 CORINTHIANS 9:8 *And God is able to make all grace (every favor and earthly blessing) come to you in abundance, so that you may always and under all circumstances and whatever the need, be self sufficient, possessing enough to require no aid or support and furnished in abundance for every good work and charitable donation. (Amplified)*	1. RECOGNIZE AND RENOUNCE THE SPIRIT OF MAMMON (Heart allegiance goes to God alone) 2. ESTABLISH SPARROW FAITH (God is my source) 3. ESTABLISH THE TITHE (Be a tither rather than just tithing) 4. BECOME GOD'S MANAGER (Become accountable to God for administration of present resources) 5. **CLOSE THE CIRCLE** (How much is enough?)

In order to learn how to practically answer in writing this question, "How much is enough," let us draw a circle, as it were, around all the money used for our personal consumption. When this question has never been answered, a family will live with what we call an **"open circle system."** Any financial increase that comes into this circle will serve only to expand the circle. A family who has answered this question will live with a **"closed circle system."** Financial increase that comes to this family will be prayed over to discover the purpose for which the Lord sent it rather than assuming that it is to be used for increasing the circle in personal consumption.

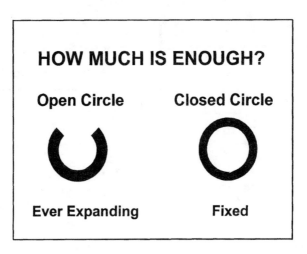

The Living Bible gives us good confirmation for this concept of the budget's being a circle in Psalm 25:12-13.

PSALM 25

12 *Where is the man who fears the Lord? God will teach him to choose the best.*

13 *He shall live within <u>God's CIRCLE of blessing</u> and his children shall inherit the earth. (TLB)*

Now, what types of things should be included inside the circle? Certainly we should include obligations and necessities. How about things we desire? Would God want to provide not only for our needs, but also for our wants? Is it legitimate for a Christian to use money for something that he/she wants that is not really a necessity, while people in other parts of the world are starving? We believe that it is God's delight and pleasure to provide His children with things that they desire, just the same as it would be for an earthly parent to do so for his/her child. However, the what and when of including wants in the circle of consumption must be decided by asking the Lord His opinion. We include a desired item in our circle, because the Lord tells us that it is the right thing and the right time to include the item, not merely because we want it and we are pressing God like a spoiled child for the money to get it.

So we are to include inside this closed circle our Obligations, Necessities and Wants. These same three items can be found in open circles also. However, those living with an open circle never know how much is enough, and consequently, as more comes to this circle, the circle expands to absorb the additional amount. In contrast, as more comes to a closed circle that has its obligations, necessities and wants predetermined, the increase bounces off as overflow and can then be directed to specific purposes. Thus, in order to answer the question "How much is enough," we have to know what our obligations, necessities and wants are now, and a projection of these three items in the short term future, such as for one year. The world system uses the term "budget" for this concept. The word budget strikes fear in some peoples' hearts. Some see a budget as an unwanted system of restrictive control over their lives. Others see it simply as something to be disregarded. In reality a budget is simply a stake in the ground with which to measure our travel through time with money. It is a way to cause money to serve us, rather than our serving Mammon through money.

Now we come to the practical details of creating a closed circle or budget. **We must answer in writing the question, "How much is enough?"** In order to understand this process, let me (Earl) tell you the story of a friend of mine. In the early 70's, my wife, Dorothy, and I were moved by the IBM Corporation to Lexington, Kentucky. I met a man, who over the years, had battled with his weight. He had a large bone structure and could carry 190 pounds well. Over the time we were there, his weight had crept up to over 320 pounds. He had been in this situation before and had tried various weight reduction methods with limited success. One day my friend noticed an ad in the newspaper, requesting people with a weight problem to participate in a university study being done on obesity. Participants were promised that this program would result in weight loss. Although skeptical, he decided to try one more program.

The first night's session, with 23 other participants, commenced with each person being given a little black book. The purpose of this book was to keep a record of everything that went into his mouth as food and drink and also record the reason why he ate or drank the item. My friend faithfully recorded all week in his book. Towards the end of the week, he noticed that some reasons were rather lame, or he no reason at all! The following Monday night, he and all the rest of the participants read out loud from their books. My friend found that he was in good company, as most of the others had also run out of reasons. The professor then collected the books and handed out yellow plastic plates and yellow cups with the following instructions. 1. The participants could eat whatever their regular menus called for and could have second helpings if they wished. 2. However, everything they ate or drank had to be eaten from the yellow plate or drunk from the yellow cup. 3. The plate must be on a table with a place setting and the proper utensils. 4. They were not allowed to watch TV or read a paper while eating if they were alone.

My friend thought to himself, "What kind of a program is this? How could anyone lose any weight by continuing to eat whatever one wants?" However, he persisted and followed the rules of the program. Whereas at night, when he normally sat in front of the TV and munched out of a bag of various types of junk foods, he now had to place his selection on a plate and eat at the table without watching the TV. At midnight when he usually raided the refrigerator, standing at the counter, with the fridge light illuminating his hands full of various food-stuffs, he now had to set a place setting and put the food on the yellow plate on the table.

After a week, he realized that this procedure was unpleasant, or as he called it, "a pain in the neck." However, he persevered and at his weekly reporting times with the group, he found something startling happening. He was losing weight. This procedure had caused him to cut out all unplanned eating. It was simply too much trouble to raid the refrigerator at night, and the snacking in front of the TV had stopped. It was too much trouble to set up a place setting for other than regular meals. His weight started to drop at the rate of 5 to

7 pounds a week! Over the months, as he continued, he brought his weight down to 190 pounds using a yellow plate and cup! I have never forgotten this story, and I immediately saw application in the area of our finances. A budget can be like a yellow plate and cup to our spending. It can eliminate all unplanned spending.

In establishing a closed circle, we will follow a similar procedure to the program for weight loss that my friend followed.

The first step is to issue yourself a "little black book," in which you will keep track of all your expenditures for a minimum of three months. You may spend whatever you like, but it must be recorded by category in the black book. There must be no leakage; all spending must be accounted for and recorded. This includes all minor cash expenditures. You may have to ask for a sales receipt, but they are available. I have a saying when you open your wallet of billfold, "Money Out— Receipts In." If the store does not automatically give you a cash register receipt, ask for one! In so doing, you are developing faithfulness in the "little." When you pay by check, always use your 'check register' to record the check number, payee, and the amount. If you use a debit card to withdraw from your bank account, record it in the same check register. If you use a credit card, keep the slips for recording purposes and reconciling your credit card statement. Each evening when you return home, you must then be diligent to record all of that day's expenditures in your record book.

An excellent book that we highly recommend for recording and then establishing a budget is called "God's Managers" by Ray and Lillian Bair, published by Herald Press in Scottsdale, Pa., 15863 USA. ISBN 0-8361-3406-0[8]. This book comes with all the recording pages necessary for 12 months of record keeping and text describing how to use the book. (see Appendix 1 for more details). There are also several good computer programs such as "Quicken," or "Microsoft Money" available for budgeting and financial tracking. However, we would recommend that you initially use the *God's Managers* hand-recorded ledger, as it already has set up for you the appropriate categories and will help you structure the Lord's tithe and your offerings.

---

[8] Ray and Lilian Bair, *God's Managers*, Herald Press, Scottdale, PA, 1985

In any case, the recording process in the book or computer should be done daily, if possible, but certainly at no interval longer than a week. Otherwise, you may tend to forget what specific receipts were for. In the God's Managers budget book, there are horizontal lines for daily entries and vertical columns for specific categories. We will list below the major categories, so that you will be able to see proposed groupings of your expenditures. A copy of the book layout is in the Appendix.

1. First fruits— tithes and offerings (giving)

2. Saving and Investment— Savings for specific wants, Kingdom purposes, Life insurance, etc.

3. Food— all types of groceries, could include dine -out; some put this in recreation.

4. Household Items -Toiletries, cleaning products, generally non-food items.

5. Housing— rent, mortgage, utilities, insurance.

6. Clothing— all items that you wear, dry cleaning

7. Transportation— car payments, gas & oil, repairs, insurance, tolls, parking etc.

8. Education— tuition, books, tapes, lessons, supplies, etc.

9. Medical and Dental— Insurance, prescriptions, supplies, personal costs.

10. Recreation— Subscriptions, hobbies, vacation, books

11. Allowances— personal pocket monies.

12. Gifts -Birthday, anniversary, Christmas, other gifts.

13. Misc.— Stationary supplies, stamps, haircuts, bank charges, etc.

14. Taxes— All deductions from paycheck,

15. Blank column for unique uses such as debt repayment.

16. Blank column for use as in 15.

17. Totals.

The **second step** is to total each column at the end of the month and record the totaled amount on the appropriate line. When all the totals are completed, then a grand total is entered. The end of the month totals are then entered on a summary page showing the totals by column and the grand total. At the end of the third month, we will have enough data to close the circle and create a budget.

The **third step** is to capture all sources of income and record the date, source and the amount. The gross amount of all salary paychecks should be entered, and the deductions taken from the amount, entered in the expense column under 'taxes.' There is a separate page to keep track of your income on a monthly basis, for a 12 month period. (See the Appendix for the page layout.) It is important that you keep track of all sources of income, so that your tithing can be correctly calculated from your gross income.

The **fourth step** is to determine what are the material wants in your life. I suggest that you make a list of all the material things that you, your spouse and family members desire. You may also include gifts with which you may wish to bless others. Put a dollar figure on each item and then prioritize the list. Have it ready for step number six.

The **fifth step** is to determine which columns in your particular situation fall into the categories of Obligations, Necessities and Wants. Each column may fall entirely into one category or may consist of more that one category of expenditures. Each person or family may have different items that are Obligations for them.

The **sixth step** is to prepare to close the circle. After three months of keeping track of your expenditures, you will have on the summary page, three numbers in each column. These numbers can be averaged for the three months. God has principles and opinions on everything that pertains to our life. He is vitally interested in our finances. Now having a record of our past spending patterns, we can ask Him about the actual numbers that we should use in each monthly column. Simply ask the Lord, "Is this number too high, too low, or correct?" Some people have to deal with fear or guilt emanating from their past when praying in this area. Some may be overly frugal and have a poverty mentality due to continual lack in childhood. Others may experience guilt as a result of unchecked over-spending, and now feel fearful of God's punishment! As we pray, we must recognize that God loves us, knows what is best for us, and He simply desires to speak to us.

If you are married, it is critical that husband and wife seek the Lord together and come into agreement over the amount for each column. If you are single, we would encourage, you to have a trusted friend with you, as together you ask the Lord for His direction for the right amount for each column. You may also wish to go through this process together with a small group, in which there is account-ability to each other. Inevitably, there will be some spiritual warfare that will take place when you first attempt to do this. Some conflict may simply arise out of selfishness in each marriage partner. Since through this process you are tearing down a major stronghold estab-lished by Mammon in your life, you can expect this spirit to power-fully resist you in closing the circle.

However, stand your ground against the enemy. I (Earl) have worked with many people, single and married, at this point of closing the circle. In doing so, I have recognized there were strongholds in these people's hearts and minds of fear, guilt, shame and many other unresolved emotional issues stemming from past experience in deal-ing with finances. This exercise frequently brings such issues to the surface. If you find a similar thing happening to you, don't be discouraged. Simply press in to God, in prayer, and seek help, if necessary. You are touching Mammon territory and the enemy does not want you free from his control in the financial realm. We inflict serious damage to the enemy, when our financial house comes into order and financial overflow begins to take place. This will then move money out of the world system and into the Kingdom of God, to be used for God's purposes of extending His Kingdom in the lives of people.

Some columns, or portions of columns, you will find to be fixed obligations. These numbers are non-optional such as mortgage payments, insurance, rent, car leases or car payments and are exam-ples of fixed obligations. Obligations are not variable and thus cannot be changed in the short term. Necessities, and wants are many times variable. There may be ways to cut back on quantity and where you buy these items. The amount should be prayed over to determine what the Lord's opinion is, in each category. So the want list that you have prepared in step four, should now be prayed over to ask the Lord what items are to be included in your circle, at this time. Recognize that His priority may be different from yours! The annual expenditure of items from your wants list that you know God has released you to include in the budget, are to be divided by 12 and entered in the savings/ investment column. Each month, money is then put aside for these items and the item purchased only when the total amount of money necessary for purchase has been accumulated. Savings may be for the replacement of a depreciating item, such as appliances or cars. There are savings set aside to bless people, through giving, as the Lord instructs you to do. If you are carrying a debt, then in your debt column, which is an obligation, you must include monies to service each debt monthly. For further discussion on debt see chapter 7.

When you have an agreed-upon amount for each column that has the Lord's approval, you can now obtain a grand total of all the columns. You now have a closed circle and have answered the question "How much is enough?" In the appendix you will find suggested percentages of the total expenses to be used as guidelines for each major category. These guidelines may be helpful if you have never had a budget before and are not familiar with the typical distribution of expenses.

I am sure your next question may be, "Does the circle ever change in size?" There may be some adjustments between or in columns, as you use the budget system. The circle should be reviewed at least once a year, or whenever your circumstances change. An example of such change would be, single to married, addition of children, other family members responsibility, relocation in a part of the country where the cost of living is different, a move to another nation, or situations that would provide a significant change in expenses. The size of the budget will reflect your particular situation and season in life. The later seasons in life when the family has grown up and left home could significantly reduce the size of the circle and provide increasing overflow for Kingdom purposes.

I'm sure you can now see why no one else can answer for you the question, "How much is enough?" The size of your circle is not a problem for God. He just wants an honest answer from you. Do you know how much is enough? It is a trust issue. God's heart is to get money into your hands, as a flow through or a channel, for His purposes in the world. Each family's financial system could be likened to a pipeline through which resources are meant to flow into the Kingdom of God. Many pipelines are plugged, and others have massive holes in the pipe, due to an open circle in that family's personal consumption. The Mammon spirit seeks to convince believers that a budget is too restrictive, too controlling. In reality, to have a closed circle is very freeing. Without a closed circle, money becomes your master and you are a slave. True freedom comes when your circle is closed. You make the decisions where your money is used and money becomes your slave. You then know where it is and what it is doing at all times! Money serves you, rather than visa versa.

When your circle is closed, you have flexibility within your own circle. If you need more money for example in the food column in a given month, you make the decision to curtail spending in other columns for a week or so and divert the money to food. At the end of the month when you total the columns you will be over budget in food, but under budget in other columns. However, the grand total remains the same and is within the overall budget. Thus money within the necessities and wants part of the circle may be reallocated, but the overall total may not be violated. If the Lord instructs you to give above what you have planned in your circle for giving, then you have the joy of making money your slave. You decide to cut back on certain expenses for that month, or to delay the purchase of some want items, thereby creating the ability to bless others and God's heart from your savings. Your Treasures in Heaven account is debited and God takes delight in flowing it back to you in multiplied form!

The seventh step is to compare your total income to the total closed circle expenses. There are three scenarios that may come from this comparison.

1. Income is less than expenditures.

2. Income is equal to expenditures.

3. Income is greater than expenditures.

Money must be prioritized and spent in the sequence of Obligations, Necessities and Wants, regardless of which scenario you find, as a result of this exercise. In the first case, it may be that there is no money for wants and only some necessities. Don't despair, this is a time to be excited, as God is in agreement with your expense side, and now faith can arise in your heart to believe God for an increase on the income side! God has creative ways to get more finances into your hands, when you have closed the circle and He is in agreement with your proposed usage of money. We encourage you to monitor your spending at the mid point of each month and compare with your budget in each column. If you notice that there is a higher demand than anticipated for that month in one column, you can then make decisions ahead of time to curtail spending in that category and reallocate money to another category. At the end of the month, you may be over budget in one column but under in others, so that you will still be within the total budget. In so doing, you are making your finances work for you.

If you have made deposits over the years in your Treasures in Heaven account, you can believe God for a release from this account. This release may come in many different ways. The Lord may influence your employer to give you a raise. He may give you a creative idea to be developed that will result in a new income stream. He may cause past investments to bear fruit. There may be a season of overtime pay, to allow you to get your debt paid off and then the money that you spent on the debt monthly will become available for other use. There may be a divine appointment with someone that results in a change of job, career, or may open an investment opportunity.

The secret is to get the circle closed, so that demonstrated faithfulness brings greater release. The trust factor is being developed between you and God over money's use, and the Mammon spirit is being defeated in your mind and heart over the consumption question. As your income begins to equal your expenses, don't stop there in your faith. It is God's purpose to continue to increase income beyond your expenditures in your life. Working through this process with God results in financial overflow.

Overflow occurs as you continue to measure your expenses to the budget numbers that have been established, and make decisions with the allocation of your money to stay within the closed circle amount. As Apostle Paul told us in 2 Corinthians, chapter 9, "God is able to make His grace abound to you," which will result in more money coming to you than the closed circle requires. God has purpose for overflow; Kingdom purpose! He may place on your heart Kingdom projects through your local church, or mission organizations. He may send you, yourself, on a mission assignment, as He provides overflow to fund all of this!

There may be a time in which God directs you to use overflow for rapid consumer debt reduction. God wants us out of debt so that we are not hindered by excessive obligations and interest payments in serving Him. The stake in the ground, or measuring stick, is the closed-circle budget. The purpose is for you to know where your money is going and for you to be making the decisions for money's direction, rather than Mammon directing you through lack, or out of control consumption, resulting in debt.

There are several areas of expenditure that we would now like to address. The first is the savings and investment area. Saving needs to be for a specific purpose. We are not meant, by God, to simply accumulate resources "for a rainy day." Saving must be designated for a specific purpose. It is legitimate for saving to be for designated for your want list, as mentioned already. Perhaps you hold a job that is paid on commission and your income fluctuates monthly. In this case, savings may be simply be monies whose purpose is to stabilize your cash flow over a period of time. If savings are not identified, one may be easily influenced by the Mammon spirit to trust in the saving's account as a source for a "rainy day." It is a subtle thing when we find ourselves starting to trust in this "nest egg" instead of trusting in the Lord as our source of provision. Having the reasons for the savings written down helps us be honest with God, that we are not trusting in our savings account. If we find that we are trusting in our savings, then we can repent and get the money properly identified.

Let us now consider the purpose and function of investing. The purpose of the investment of money is to cause money to work for us in the creation of riches. Money can be placed in investment opportunities that are offered in the world system, such as stocks, bonds, mutual funds, etc. The purpose of the investments made also must be identified for the same reasons mentioned regarding savings. Some of those funds could be identified for increasing fruits of righteousness (see Chapter 8). Other funds may be set aside for Kingdom work, to be accessed when the Lord calls for them. We see an example of assets, which were available to the Lord when He called for them in Matthew 21.

MATTHEW 21

1   And when they came near Jerusalem and had reached
    Bethphage, at the Mount of Olives, Jesus sent two disciples
    on ahead.

2   *Saying to them, Go into the village that is opposite you, and*
    a once you will find a donkey tied and a colt with her; untie
    her and bring them to Me.

3   *If any one says anything to you, you shall reply,* <u>The Lord</u>
    <u>*needs them,*</u> *and he will let them go without delay.*
    (Amplified)

The owner of these animals apparently understood that they were to be available to the Lord for a specific purpose. God will place in your heart a knowing that certain investments are for Kingdom purposes. When the Lord calls for them, you will know to release the funds for His purposes. These funds could be held in "the Master has need of account!" There may be funds that are for sowing and reaping purposes in the Kingdom, in which you are to sow into a Kingdom ministry, or project and believe God for a multiplied return for a larger Kingdom purpose. (See Chapter 9 for further amplification).

Let us now share with you some thoughts that may speak to you in the area of buying and selling, versus giving and receiving. I (Earl) was involved in helping a YWAM staff person establish a closed circle. In her closed circle, she had placed some money monthly into a savings account to be used for the purchase of a camera. She planned to purchase the camera when the account reached $250, the cost of the camera. As the account approached that amount, this staff member prayed, just to confirm with the Lord that she should now purchase of this item. However, even though she now had the money, she sensed from the Lord that she was to wait until a later time for this purchase.

Two weeks later a man can into the YWAM office holding a bag of camera equipment, which he wished to donate to the ministry. He asked me if I knew of anyone in our ministry who needed a camera. I directed this man to our staff girl. She received the camera bag and found over $750 worth of camera equipment in the bag. She now had a camera of greater function and value than her $250 would have purchased and still had the money that had been saved! When she prayed about her savings money, the Lord told her to give it to another person who was believing God for a financial release for another purpose. Look with me at how Kingdom finances functioned in this transaction.

The man who gave the camera equipment had a deposit made into his Treasures in Heaven account for its value, $750. The girl received a camera worth three times the value of what she was saving for. Her giving of the saved money was then deposited in her Treasures in Heaven account, in the amount of $250. This account was then multiplying, ready to supply her closed circle in the coming days. Now contrast this with the transaction in the world system, had it taken place. She would have gone to a camera store and placed $250 on the counter and received a camera for that value. Transaction completed.

Instead, $1,000 was deposited in the Treasures in Heaven accounts of believers multiplying for a return to them in the future. Thus there is a multiplication in giving and receiving that does not occur in buying and selling. This is the mechanism of Kingdom finances. Buying and selling is not wrong, but God may have higher purposes to be accomplished in these types of transactions through giving and receiving. The moral is, don't jump too quickly in purchasing items, even when you have the money. Ask the Lord!

CHAPTER 7
STEP UP TO YOUR DEBT

JOHN 4:23-24

SPIRIT	TRUTH
Faith *Romans 10:17* Word	Faith *Luke 17:5-10* Obedience
GRACE	**BUILDING BLOCKS**
2 CORINTHIANS 9:8	1. RECOGNIZE AND RENOUNCE THE SPIRIT OF MAMMON
And God is able to make all grace (every favor and earthly blessing) come to you in abundance, so that you may always and under all circumstances and whatever the need, be self sufficient, possessing enough to require no aid or support and furnished in abundance for every good work and charitable donation. (Amplified)	(Heart allegiance goes to God alone)
	2. ESTABLISH SPARROW FAITH
	(God is my source)
	3. ESTABLISH THE TITHE
	(Be a tither rather than just tithing)
	4. BECOME GOD'S MANAGER
	(Become accountable to God for administration of present resources)
	5. CLOSE THE CIRCLE
	(How much is enough?)
	6. STEP UP TO YOUR DEBT
	(Acknowledge and properly deal with all debt)

Before we continue talking about the five scriptural uses of money from Second Corinthians chapter 9, let us in this chapter address the issue of debt. Western society is riddled with debt. People in our generation seem to be drunk on and consumed with debt. Most people have come to accept that living with significant consumer, corporate, and national debt is a normal way of life. However, we do not believe that this is normal. It is just common. Common is not necessarily normal.

It has not always been that way in the United States or any of the other western countries. In the United States, it took over 200 years, form 1776 to 1980, to accumulate the first trillion dollars of national debt. How long do you think it took to double that and accumulate the second trillion? The United States was able to accomplish this in only six years. In 1986 we hit the second trillion dollars of debt. By 1990 the United States had accumulated its third trillion, and by 1994, we were over five trillion dollars in debt. At the turn of the millennium the national debt was well in excess of eight trillion dollars. One doesn't have to be an economist or mathematician to understand that any individual or economic unit that continues to spend more resource than it generates will eventually collapse.

After a lecture by a university professor on economics, an old farmer was asked if he had understood the concepts explained in the professor's lecture. Old Amos replied, "Yes sir, I sure do. The professor said, **'If your out-go exceeds your income, your upkeep is gonna be your downfall.'**" This is very simple, right? Apparently not, for many families, corporations, and nations.

The biblical prophet Haggai addressed this problem.

HAGGAI 1

5   *Now therefore thus says the Lord of hosts; 'Consider your ways!*

6   *You have sown much and bring in little. You eat, but you do not have enough. You drink, but you are not filled with drink. You clothe yourselves, but no one is warm. And he who earns wages, earns wages to be put into a bag with holes.'*

7   *Thus says the Lord of hosts; 'Consider your ways.' (NKJV)*

Many who read this scripture feel that it is the story of their lives. They never have enough. It is as if the bag into which all their money is put has holes in it. It all leaks out as fast as they put it in. The Lord here encourages us to consider our ways. Most people first of all check their conduct to see if what they are doing is right. They then check their motive to see if the reason why they're doing it is right. If they find that what they're doing is O.K., and why they're doing it is O.K., they usually conclude that everything is fine. However, the Lord here in this passage brings up another area to check, the ways. "**Consider your ways**," says the Lord.

Kingdom order in any individual's finances is prosperity, provision and freedom from debt. Unplanned debt is a lack of connection between the debtor and his God as provider. Unplanned debt, by definition, is a breakdown in the order of the Kingdom of God in a believer's life. The order and authority of God reflected in an individual's finances is that there will be enough provision to meet each necessity at the appropriate time. Many times it is neither what we are doing that is wrong, nor the motive for doing it, but rather the way or timing in doing it. We do the right thing with the right motive at the wrong time or in the wrong way. We believe that the way many people use debt is one of these ways that is destructive.

Many people never stop to actually consider the total cost of an item purchased on credit. Here is a fact that would shock and horrify most people. What percentage of a person's lifetime income would you think might be spent on paying interest on debt? The average North American will make between $1,000,000 and $5,000,000 in the course of his/her career between ages twenty and sixty-five. **Most of these people will spend between one half and two thirds of their lifetime income servicing their debt.** Who in their right mind would set out in the beginning of their career to spend 50% to 67% of their lifetime earnings on interest to service debt?

With this kind of money being given to bankers, mortgage companies and credit card companies, can you see how the body of Christ, at large, is being robbed? Imagine what we could do if just half of this money that is being poured into interest would be redirected into the Kingdom of God. How much of the money you pay in interest do you really think finds its way into the Kingdom of God to effectively accomplish Kingdom work? Why does this happen? I believe that the primary reason so much of our income is directed into paying interest is that we have not really thought through how we spend our money.

As we consider debt in this chapter, we would first like to identify four different types of debt: 1) consumer debt, 2) mortgage debt, 3) business debt, and investment debt. It is beyond the scope of this book to deal to any extent with business debt and investment debt. Here we will primarily be discussing consumer debt and, to a small extent, mortgage debt. This leads us to an obvious question. **Is all debt wrong?** No, not categorically. Incurring debt is not inherently sinful, as some would think, but often is simply unwise. In certain cases, incurring debt is sinful and is called by the Bible wicked. We will talk about this a little later in this chapter. Unless specifically noted, from this point forward in this chapter when we are talking about debt, we are talking specifically about personal, consumer debt.

Because everything in western society is sold to us on weekly or monthly payments, most people do not stop to think about the total cost of any purchase they make. People rarely stop to ask the question, "How much am I actually paying for that? I'm buying something that's advertised to be $1,000, but if I purchase on credit, how much will I actually pay for the item?" Frequently, you will pay one and a half or two times the purchase price if interest is included. Thus, you may pay $1,500 or $2,000 for a $1,000 item. If people really thought this through in advance, very few would choose to pay double for something. The problem is that most people do not think this through in advance.

When we look back at the scripture in Haggai 1:5, we can see that the hole in many peoples' bags is the interest they pay on all the items they have purchased. Here God is calling us to consider our ways. Is this really the right way to do things?

For example, if you were to purchase a $100,000 house with a thirty-year mortgage at eight and a half percent interest, how much would you pay in total over the course of the thirty years? The amount would be approximately $275,000. If one were to add back into the equation the taxes paid on the $275,000 one would have to earn something on the order of $400,000 in order to pay for a $100,000 house in this way. How many people would do this if they had really thought through in advance the total cost of their house? Many people cannot see any other way to do this. Again, this is why Haggai tells us to consider our ways.

I believe that for some people the strongholds regarding debt that the spirit of Mammon has established in their minds is generational. It is the way their parents and perhaps even grandparents have thought and conducted their financial affairs. Again, Proverbs 22:6 tells us to "Train up a child in the way he should go, and when he is old he will not depart from it." Many people, through observation of their own parents, have been trained up in the ways of incurring debt, and now in their adulthood they have not departed from these ways. They don't know of any other way.

I believe that for many people there is a significant deception involved in their incurring debt. Let's look at Genesis 3:13. This is the account of Adam and Eve in the Garden of Eden. After the man and woman had partaken of the fruit of the tree of the knowledge of good and evil, God confronted the woman, "And the Lord God said to the woman, "What is this that you have done?" And the woman said, "The serpent beguiled me, and I ate." (Genesis 3:13) I want to take a closer look at the Hebrew word translated in this passage "beguiled" or "deceived." This is the Hebrew word "*Nasha*," which actually is a homonym in Hebrew. *Nasha* has two meanings. One meaning is to deceive or beguile, while the other meaning is to lend at interest.[9]

So, what in reality did the serpent do to Eve? He drew her into spiritual debt, in which the interest was running so rapidly, she could never catch up and pay it off in a lifetime. It took God Almighty, Himself, Incarnate in the Lord Jesus Christ, to pay Adam and Eve's debt. There was no way she nor anyone else on planet earth could pay the interest on the debt that she incurred through that deception, through that beguilement. Now, isn't it interesting that the same

---

[9] James Strong, *Strong's Exhaustive Concordance of the Bible*, Baker Book House, Grand Rapids, Michigan 1985, n.d. *nasha* (# H 5377,5378)

word in Hebrew used for deception is the word that is used for lending money at interest. Why are people flocking to sign up to purchase all kinds of things on credit? We believe that it is this same deceptive spirit working in peoples' lives today.

When people are in bondage to the spirit of Mammon, they don't think before they act. Again, many people never calculate how much something actually costs. They're just looking at the monthly payment, instead of the total cost of the item. Another very interesting word in Hebrew relating to debt is the word *"nashak,"*[10] (Strong's Concordance number 5391). This word literally means, "to strike with a sting (as a serpent)." We see this word used in Numbers 21:8-9 regarding literally being bitten by poisonous snakes.

NUMBERS 21

8   *Then the Lord said to Moses, 'Make a fiery serpent (of bronze), and set it on a pole; and it shall be that everyone who is bitten* (nashak)*, when he looks at it, shall live.'*

9   *So Moses made a bronze serpent, and put it on a pole; and if a serpent had bitten* (nashak) *anyone, when he looked at the bronze serpent, he lived." (NKJV)*

So in this passage, *nashak* means to be bitten by a literal poisonous snake. The figurative meaning of this same word *nashak* is to oppress with interest on a loan, or to lend upon usury. It is interesting that again this same word has a double meaning. We see this usage in the passage in Deuteronomy 23:20. "You shall not charge interest (*nashak*) to your brother— interest on money or food or anything that is lent out at interest." Literally this passage says, "You shall not bite your brother as a snake."

We see this same meaning of the word *nashak* again in Habakkuk 2:7.

---

[10] James Strong, *Strong's Exhaustive Concordance of the Bible*, Baker Book House, Grand Rapids, Michigan 1985, n.d. *nashak* (# H 5391)

HABAKKUK 2

7   *Will not your creditors* (snakebiters) *rise up suddenly?*
Will they not awaken who oppress you? And you will become
their booty. (NKJV)

The King James version translates this passage as follows:

HABAKKUK 2

7   *"Shall they not rise up suddenly <u>that shall bite thee,</u> and*
awake that shall vex thee, and thou shalt be for booties unto
them." (KJV)

So, apparently at that time they did not have loan sharks, but
rather loan snakes. Thus, in looking at these two Hebrew words,
nasha (to beguile or deceive) and *nashak* (to bite as a poisonous
snake), we see that the spirit of Mammon has a function to deceive
and to bite as a snake in enticing people to live a lifestyle based on
debt and paying large percentages of income to interest. What the
serpents were doing to the people in the wilderness, turns out to be
the same as what the money changers and lenders were doing to
people later in Israel's history. They were siding with the spirit of
Mammon to use money to oppress people. I believe this again is
what incensed Jesus and compelled Him to drive the money-changers
out of the court of grace in the temple. I don't believe that Jesus was
really driving out the people as much as He was driving out the spirit.
I'm sure that the money-changers were not exchanging at an even
rate. The spirit of Mammon saw to it that there was usury involved.

I'd like to share with you a part of a poem, entitled, "The First
Mortgage." This poem exemplifies the meaning of *nashak*, regarding
the Garden of Eden.

THE FIRST MORTGAGE [11]

"In this land there ne'er was a weed,
The plants that grew came not from seed;
The will of God had placed them there,
Tempered the breeze, and the balmy air.

Flowers of every shade and hue,
The red and orange, white and blue,
With mosses growing on the trees,
And vines that swayed with every breeze.

The mellow light from the midnight moon,
Rays so bright from the sun at noon,
The sweet perfume and singing birds
Cannot be told in human words.

As down the flowery isles they walked,
Of love's young dream together they talked,
How quickly must the years have sped
When Eve and Adam first were wed.

To him it was a world of joys,
No jealousy of other boys
No pangs to cause his soul unrest,
For fear she loved another best.

And thus they did each other please,
'Till Eve went shopping "mongst the trees;
And wished some applesauce to make,
And got the apples of a snake.

When Adam came that night to tea,
She said "Here's applesauce for thee."
She'd made it very nice and sweet,
So Adam took it and did eat.

---

[11] E. U. Cook, *The First Mortgage*, Rhodes and McClure Publishing Co., Chicago, 1898, pp.19-21

And on its goodness she enlarged,
Because, no doubt, she'd had it "charged."
And then perhaps besides the fruit,
She may have bought a fig-leaf suit.

And just as other merchants will,
The snake at last came with his bill;
And Adam then refused to pay,
And tried to send the snake away.

And enmity the Lord did make,
Between the woman and the snake,
And enmity the Lord did quoth,
Should be between the seed of both.

"And it shall bruise the serpent's head,
And thou shalt bruise his heal instead:"
And here the promise first is met,
Of His who came to pay the debt.

And while the snake around him lurked,
The devil came for whom he clerked,
And then he said to make me whole,
"I'll take a mortgage on your soul."

And then a mortgage Adam gives,
On every soul that ever lives;
And when that mortgage was arranged,
How quickly everything was changed.

Disease and sickness, grief and pain,
Shadow and sorrow, drought and rain,
Discord and murder, every sin,
Were by this mortgage ushered in.

The storm-winds blew and not the breeze,
The wild birds screamed amongst the trees,
The rag-weeds and the foxtail grew,
The cuckle-burr and thistle, too.

Now Adam to supply his needs,
Hoed the garden and mowed the weeds,
He tilled the soil through drought and wet-
You should have seen that old man sweat!

All through the day ol' Adam ploughs,
And then goes home and milks the cows,
And feeds the pigs and little fowls,
And then sits round and growls and growls.

A bitter follows all his sweets,
A foe for every friend he meets;
The hawks do on the sparrows prey,
The tall trees and the tempests sway.

The word mortgage is actually a very interesting word. It is originally a French word, stemming from two other words. "Mort," which means death in French, and "gage," which means a measure, or portion. **So a mortgage, then, is a measure or portion of death.** It has never occurred to most people that there would be any other way to acquire a house other than by taking a long-term mortgage at interest. Is it categorically wrong to incur debt? There are many examples of debt in Scripture. In Deuteronomy 28:12b "...and you shall lend to many nations, but you shall not borrow." If borrowing was a sin, then, God was instructing nations to sin as they borrowed from Israel. We don't think so. In 2 Kings 4:1-7, a widow of a prophet's son was in terrible debt, so much so that she feared her creditors would take her two sons to be slaves. She was instructed by the prophet Elisha to borrow vessels in order that a miracle, which would be used to get her out of debt, could take place. Sometimes it is necessary to borrow to get out of debt. This is particularly true when that which is borrowed will produce positive cash flow. You need wisdom from God and wise counsel in this matter.

There is, however, a tremendous deception involved with debt and a door that is opened to the spirit of Mammon. Let us share with you a simple truth. If most people were to simply accelerate the payment of the mortgage on their house, they could eliminate it in seven years or less, and save many tens of thousands of dollars in interest.

Let us give you an example, using some statistics from a typical U.S. situation. If you live in another country, your numbers may be different, but the principle will be the same. These statistics are using mortgage interest rates of about 8 ½%, and credit card rates of around 16% to 19%. If you live in an economy, in which the rates are higher than these, then the situation is even more severe in your case.

Using the following U.S. numbers, by utilizing only 10% of monthly income to accelerate debt payment, the average American household could save $105,000 in interest and build over $1,200,000 in investments in the same time it would have taken just to pay off their house. We will use averages as they were reported in 1994. These absolute numbers may have grossly changed by now, but the principle is the same. The numbers used in the example below were originally compiled by John Cummuta, and presented in his course, *Debt Free and Prosperous Living.*[12] Now, here's the example. Let's take a sample household that has the following income and debt scenario.

1. Annual Household Income: $47,221
    ($3935/month gross income, $2951 net income)
    Source: US Census Bureau, Division of Income Analysis 1994

2. Mortgage: Balance: $87,000
    Monthly Payment (w/o tax, insurance): $662
    Interest: 8.24%
    Source: National Association of Realtors, 1994
    Length of Loan Remaining: 28.4 years
    Source: Chicago Title and Trust of Title Insurers, 1994

3. Credit Card Debt: Total Balance: $3,300
    Source: Bankcard Holders of America, 1995
    Sample Breakout:
    MasterCard $1,425 balance; ($36/mo.min. @ 17%)
    VISA $1,250 balance; ($32/mo.min. @ 16 1/2%)

---

[12] John Commuta, *Debt Free and Prosperous Living*, Wauzeka, Wisconsin, Marketline Press Sixth Edition, 1994

| Discover | $655 balance; ($18/mo. min. @ 19.8%) |

4. Car Loans:
   His Car Loan: $7,250 balance; ($212/mo. @ 12.9%)
   Her Car Loan: $5,500 balance; ($125/mo. @ 13.8%)

5. Home Equity Loan: $5,000 balance; ($125/mo. @ 9.6%)

Total Monthly Payments: $1,230 (31.3% of gross income)

If this family simply paid their minimum payments, in 28.4 years they would own their house free and clear and would own some really old cars. Suppose, instead, that this family tightened their belts and allocated 10% of their monthly gross income ($390) to accelerate their debt payment. Here is what could happen.

This family could:

1. Be totally debt free in 7 years and 6 months (20 years 10 months faster than normal).

2. Save $105,408 in interest not paid to creditors.

3. Have a six-month cash reserve: $10,326 = 6 months x ($2,951, net income— $1,230 former debt payment)

4. Have an additional, passive, monthly cash flow of **$10,326/mo.** by investing the liberated $1,620/mo. ($1,230 former debt payment + $390 10% Debt Accelerator) for the remaining 20 years 4 months at a 10% rate of return. This would yield **$1,278,260, the interest on which @ 10% would pay $10,326/month for life.**

Suppose this family instead allocated 20% of their monthly gross income ($780 to accelerate their debt payment.) In this case, this family could:

1. Be totally debt free in 5 years and 7 months (22 years, 9 months faster than normal).

2. Save $115,928 in interest not paid to creditors.

3. Have a six-month cash reserve: $10,326 = 6 months x ($2,951, net income— $1,230 former debt payment)

4. Have an additional, passive, monthly cash flow of $15,909/mo. by investing the liberated $2,010/mo. ($1,230 former debt payment + $780 10% Debt Accelerator) for the remaining 22 years 4 months at a 10% rate of return. This would yield $1,988,686, the interest on which @ 10% would pay **$15,909/month for life.**

Now which one of these scenarios would be wiser? Would you rather have at the end of 28.4 years a house free and clear, or a house free and clear, and $1,278,260 invested, yielding $10,226 per month in interest, and a six-month cash reserve?

In the above scenario, we are simply talking about reversing interest in the world system. We have not yet started talking about multiplication in the Kingdom of God. We're only talking about reversing percentage increase in the world system, to make it go the other way; to make it go for you instead of against you. This is not beyond the reach of most people. Many people, if they applied a little discipline to their lives, could do this.

Let us give you another example of the simple power of compound interest. Again, this is just percentage increase in the world system, not multiplication in the Kingdom of God. If you started at age 15, and invested a certain sum of money every day at a ten percent return, how much would the daily sum need to be to reach a total of $1,000,000 at age 60? What if you started at a later age? Here is a chart showing these numbers:

Daily Amount Necessary @ 10% to Yield $1 Million at Age 60

Age	Daily Investment	Total Principal Invested
15	$.50	$8,213
20	$1.00	$14,600
30	$5.00	$54,750
40	$21.67	$158,191
50	$116.67	$425,845

Again, how difficult would this be for most people? Whom do you know who could not invest $.50 per day? Virtually no one. This is easy to do. Why do most people not do this? Two reasons: 1. It is easier not to do. 2. "For lack of knowledge my people perish." (Hosea 4:6) Many people simply did not realize the power of interest, either for or against them. We are not talking at all yet about the supernatural power of managing resources in God's Kingdom. We are simply talking about reversing interest in the world system.

CREDIT CARD DEBT

Some might ask, "What about using credit cards? Is this wrong?" We would answer that it is not categorically wrong to use credit cards. However, we believe that credit cards should never be used for credit. I (Craig) have used credit cards for most of my adult life, and still do today. However, I have never incurred a finance charge on a credit card, except one time when I mistakenly neglected to send in a payment on time. I pay the full balance due on any card I use by the due date each month. Jan and I made the commitment years ago that in any month we are not able to do so, we will cut up the card and terminate its usage. A credit card should be used as if it were cash that you had in your wallet. It must be backed by money in your account so it can be paid in full monthly.

If carrying credit cards leads you to violate your closed-circle budget, we highly suggest that you cut up your cards and terminate their usage. If this strikes fear in your heart, that alone ought to be an indicator to you of what spirit is even now influencing your thoughts and emotions. If you are relying on a credit card for emergencies rather than relying on God, you might consider in whom you are trusting.

A GOOD MAN LEAVES AN INHERITANCE

When considering the purchase of a home, the best situation would be to own a home with no mortgage at all. If suggested, however, most people would consider this to be an impossibility. How could a couple of newlyweds in their early twenties ever be able to afford to purchase a house outright for cash with no mortgage? By themselves, they could not. However, I don't believe that God ever intended for us to walk through life by ourselves. I believe that God intended for there to be financial blessing passed down from generation to generation.

Proverbs 13:22 states that a good man leaves an inheritance to his children's children. One man I know found an interesting way to leave a generational inheritance for his children and grandchildren. He had prospered quite well in business and had decided, as his oldest daughter was ready to marry, to purchase the newlyweds a house. Because of the overflow with which God had blessed him in his own life, he was able to purchase the house with cash. This father then made the following proposition to his son-in-law and daughter. He asked them to pay him a monthly payment equal to a typical mortgage payment, which he would then invest in an interest-bearing account. They were to make these payments for twenty years, at which time the father would then convey title to the house to the young couple. The sum of money that had accumulated and grown in the interest-bearing account was then to be used to purchase a house for the grandchildren who would be nearing the age of marrying and needing a house twenty years hence. The same requirement was then to be placed upon the grandchildren who would pay into an interest-bearing account to create the ability to buy a house outright for the great grandchildren again twenty years hence. In this way, this father set up a perpetual system of blessing each generation with a house without ever being charged interest or becoming encumbered with a mortgage.

In modern society, usually the inheritance is passed to the children rather than to the grandchildren, as Proverbs 13:22 suggests. However, think about this. How old are the children typically when the parents usually pass away? Perhaps fifty or sixty. How old are the grandchildren? Maybe twenty or thirty. Would most people be more in need of a financial inheritance at age fifty or at age twenty? Obviously at age twenty. If we would follow the scriptural pattern of each generation's giving an inheritance to the grandchildren rather than to the children, each generation could avoid the interest most people pay in their twenties and thirties as they are just starting out. God revealed Himself as the God of Abraham, Isaac, and Jacob. That is the three-generation principle.

Dennis Peacocke in his book *"Doing Business God's Way,"*[13] talks about the relational stewardship that God wants to instill in each of His children toward faithful stewardship of wealth and responsibilities, whether physical or spiritual. He lists three elements: 1) receiving an inheritance, 2) preserving and building that inheritance, and 3) passing that inheritance on to future generations. According to George Guilder, "The vast majority of American's fortunes are dissipated within two generations." The curse of poverty is single generational wealth. It is selfishness versus heritage, or consumption versus savings.

We believe that it is important to recognize that debt does not just affect the natural realm, but also the spiritual realm. We believe that there is literally a demonic spirit of debt that couples with the spirit of Mammon to create incredible emotional and spiritual pressure in the lives of those whom it afflicts. Many times debt can create an overwhelming sense of hopelessness, shame, and fear. The feeling we have had many people describe is likened to drowning and gasping for air. Many people are emotionally paralyzed by debt. These emotional pressures can often times result in physical sickness, mental distress, and marital breakdown in a family.

As a result of these types of pressures, many people in their emotional paralysis, hide from their creditors, and do not act in integ-

---

[13]Dennis Peacocke, *Doing Business God's Way*, REBUILD, Santa Rosa California 1995, pages34-39.

rity by simply communicating. This then worsens the situation and causes the creditors to pursue the debtor with a vengeance. Often in a marriage, because the husband is now working three jobs in an attempt to be a good provider and meet his debt obligations, his wife is left to deal with the creditors who call or stop by to attempt to collect on the debt. Many times this results in pressure coming upon the wife that she was never designed by God to have to deal with. As this pressure increases, so does marital strife, anger and relational breakdown between husband and wife. We believe in this case that the husband is truly shirking his responsibility, as the priest of his home, to step up to his debt and personally communicate with each of the creditors, so that this burden does not fall on his wife.

For many people, the taking on of destructive debt is a generational pattern. How did people get the idea to use credit cards for immediate gratification of desires? Many times it was learned from parents.

PROVERBS 22

6 *Train up a child in the way he should go, and when he is old, he will not depart.*

7 *The rich rule over the poor and the borrower is slave to the lender. (NKJV)*

Many people have not correlated verse 7 of Proverbs 22 with the preceding verse. I believe that understanding this master/slave relationship regarding debt is one of the first principles that a wise father will teach his sons and daughters. However, many times just the opposite is modeled. Children learn to use debt to instantly gratify their desires, rather than waiting on God for His timing and provision. Their parents trained them up in the way they should go, and when they are old, they do not depart.

Now is debt categorically wrong? Is it something that you should never incur? No, we don't believe that it is categorically wrong. Many times it is simply not wisdom to incur debt on depreciating or consumable items, but it is not necessarily sinful. However, it is important to realize that when one opens the door to debt, he/she potentially opens the door to demonic activity in the spirit realm. It is not just a financial transaction, but is also a spiritual transaction. One will have to deal with the Mammon spirit, which will try to deceive, entice, and seduce. Many Christians seem to be unaware of this.

DEAL WITH YOUR OWN WICKEDNESS

PSALM 37

21 The wicked borrows and does not repay, but the righteous shows mercy and gives. (NKJV)

Now, what is the person called who borrows with no means to repay according to the Bible? This person is called "wicked." Although debt is not categorically wrong or sinful, to borrow and not repay is. Many people just sign their name on a credit card slip with no idea of how they are going to pay. The Bible calls this person "wicked." We want to look now at a specific area in which many people become unintentionally wicked. This has to do with the aspect of loans made to family members or close friends.

Many times parents or other family members lend each other money with the provision, "Pay us back when you can." Now, let me ask you, when does "when you can" come? It usually comes on the Twelfth of Never. Some of the most frequent perpetrators of this are parents with a good intention in their hearts lending money to their grown children. Without realizing it, these parents have hung a millstone of debt around the neck of their children by lending them money with no provision to retire the debt. Without realizing it, they have opened the door in the lives of their children to the spirit of Mammon. The children usually feel in this type of loan that they must have the entire amount to pay back to their parents, which, of course, never happens.

For example, suppose that parents lend their son and daughter-in-law $10,000 with the provision, "pay us back when you can." Usually the children are waiting for a time when they have $10,000, which they can return to their parents. Of course, this never happens, so they never make any payment on their debt at all. Usually as time goes on, this situation begins to affect the relationship between borrower and lender. If no payment is ever made on the loan, after a period of time, the lender begins to feels feelings of resentment. Suppose the children take their family on a vacation and spend $2,000. The parents may feel as follows. "How do they have $2,000 to go on a vacation, but they can't even pay $100 toward retiring the debt they owe us?"

Perhaps the parents never say anything to the children, but an emotional undertone is created in the relationship. The children feel the resentment of the parents, and they begin to feel guilty. Because of the emotional undertones, neither the parents nor the children now enjoy spending time together. They each feel uncomfortable in each other's presence, and the spirit of Mammon then couples with areas of iniquity in the hearts of each and successfully breaks down the relationship. This family no longer wants to spend Christmas or other holidays together. Each time they see each other there is the underlying guilt and resentment.

Now the parents in this case had a good intention in their hearts to help their children, but simply did so in the wrong way. (Haggai 1:7; "Thus says the Lord of hosts, 'Consider your ways.'") They did not use God's wisdom in their desire to help their children. What would have been a way to help the children in wisdom? I believe first of all that it is critical for potential lenders to diligently seek God as to whether God really wants them to lend or not. Another option would be to simply give the money as a gift, with no expectation of repayment whatsoever. However, if the Lord is leading you to lend to someone, especially a family member, it is important that the loan be structured with repayment terms. Now you should lend the money without charging interest, but you must set up a payment schedule and hold the borrower accountable to meet it. The Bible correctly tells us that the borrower becomes a servant to the lender (Proverbs 22:7). Thus, the borrower, before he/she receives the loan, must be in agreement with the repayment terms and the consequences for failure to do so.

How does one rectify this situation if money has already been lent with no repayment terms? Let's look at this from both the side of the lender as well as the borrower. From the borrower's stand-point, the first thing to be done is to repent before God of wickedness. Secondly, the borrower must then look at his/her own closed circle budget, seek the Lord and determine what money is available to begin to pay on a monthly basis toward the debt. After this determination has been made, the borrower can go to the lender, confess the wickedness of borrowing and not repaying, and present a payment plan to begin to retire the debt. In this way the borrower is stepping up to his/her debt and properly dealing with it. Even when the initial monthly amount that can be paid is very small compared to the entire amount of the debt, beginning to do what one can breaks the stronghold of the spirit of Mammon and debt. This then releases God to perform the supernatural in the life of the debtor.

Let's now look at this from the standpoint of the lender. If you have lent money with no specific terms, you have violated the world system. We must remember that money belongs to the world system. The rules that govern money are established by the banks. As Christians, we have already determined that we are to be faithful stewards of that which belongs to another (Luke 16:12). The rules of the world system in handling debt require a minimum or an agreed monthly payment. We cannot violate this rule and expect the Lord to override this violation. Even God respects what truly belongs to the devil. However, if we have met the rules that govern money, we can ask God to override with Kingdom principles in our situations.

If no effort has been made on the part of the debtor to repay, the lender must first seek the Lord, and ask the question, "Is this really meant to be a debt, and I need to hold the borrower account-able, or should I make this a gift and release the debtor from the obligation to repay?" If the lender feels that the Lord is directing to forgive the debt, he/she can then go to the borrower, repent of placing him/her in debt with no specific terms and offer to forgive the debt. If the lender feels to hold the borrower accountable to pay the debt, then he/she should go to the borrower and repent of plac-ing him/her in debt with no specific terms. He/she may then ask to sit down and help the debtor determine from his/her closed-circle or budget what amount can reasonably be paid on the debt each month.

If the borrower refuses to come to an agreement or refuses to pay on the debt, the lender should follow the procedures outlined by Jesus in Matthew 18 regarding a brother who has sinned against you.

MATTHEW 18

15 *Moreover if your brother sins against you, go and tell him his fault between you and him alone. If he hears you, you have won your brother.*

16 *But if he will not hear, take with you one or two more, that by the mouth of two or three witnesses every word may be established.*

17 *And if he refused to hear them, tell it to the church. But if he refuses even to hear the church, let him be to you like a heathen and a tax collector. (NKJV)*

This procedure would apply to any Christian to whom money has been lent, not just to family members. The purpose of this process is to allow the Lord maximum opportunity to deal with the hearts of both parties. It may be irresponsible to just release the debtor from the debt when the Lord wants to use the circumstance to deal with the heart. Many times the Lord will also deal with the heart of the lender through this process. Let us examine the practical implementation of this scripture. After confronting the debtor personally, if there is no resolution, then the next step is to involve spiritual authority as witnesses. I believe that this means to bring the case to the pastor of the debtor and the lender. If one party has no pastor, then involve whomever he/she would honor as a godly person from whom he/she would receive input. If there were no resolution brought on this level, we would recommend contacting the Peacemakers International (www.hispeace.org), which has developed a wonderful procedure of mediation/arbitration to settle such disputes. This type of service is available in a number of countries.

After following this procedure Jesus outlines in Matthew 18, the lender may still choose to forgive the debt and release the debtor. It would never be right to pursue civil, legal action against another Christian.

1 CORINTHIANS 6

6   *But brother goes to law against brother, and that before unbelievers. Now therefore, it is already an utter failure for you that you go to law against one another. Why do you not rather accept wrong? Why do you not rather let yourselves be cheated? (NKJV)*

MATTHEW 5

40   *If anyone wants to sue you and take away your tunic, let him have your cloak also. (NKJV)*

The concept of "letting him have your cloak also" is so that we can move into Kingdom principles. The world system wants to extract from you. The Kingdom of God operates on the principle of giving and receiving. Thus there is a releasing and then a giving to break through in the spirit realm over this situation.

STEP UP TO YOUR DEBT

Let's now discuss the concept of stepping up to one's debt. As we mentioned earlier, one of the major problems associated with debt is the emotional fear, shame, worthlessness, and paralysis that accompanies major consumer debt. This causes people to hide from their creditors and not communicate. Stepping up to debt entails taking responsibility for the debt incurred and communicating with creditors in integrity. The first step in stepping up to debt is to repent before the Lord for the wickedness of borrowing without means to repay, if this is the case. The blood of Jesus was shed to remove the guilt and defilement stemming from this area of sin.

Secondly, a major paradigm shift must take place for most people who find themselves in a position of overwhelming debt. When you are in this position, the spirit of Mammon frequently keeps your focus on what you don't have and what you can't do. **You must purposefully refocus on what you do have and what you can do.** God cannot do anything with what you don't have. He can work only with what you do have. When you begin to do what can naturally be done, God is released to do what He can do supernaturally. Every miracle is a combination of a man/woman's doing natural things coupled with God's doing supernatural things.

When Peter in the Bible walked on the water, he had to do a very natural thing. He was required to climb over the side of the boat and walk. This was not supernatural. He had been daily climbing over the sides of boats and walking for years. The supernatural part of this miracle was that God supported Peter on water. If Peter had not done his natural part, the miracle could not have taken place. Likewise if God had not done His supernatural part, the miracle could not have taken place. Both parts were essential. If Peter had continued to focus on what he could not do (support himself on water), he would have been paralyzed and never moved to do his natural part. Remember, eleven others sat in the boat waiting for God to do something. Many people sit paralyzed with overwhelming debt praying and waiting for God to do something. Miracles are released when we do the natural part and trust God for the supernatural part. So we must start by focusing on what we do have and what we can do. When we do the natural, then God is released to do the supernatural. Don't be like one of the other eleven disciples, sitting in the boat waiting for God to do something.

When Jesus fed the five thousand (John 6:1-14), His disciples were focusing on that which they did not have, namely, food. Jesus changed their focus to look at what was available. When they presented to Jesus the one lunch that the young boy had available, Jesus multiplied it supernaturally. Doing the natural is always the first step in releasing the supernatural.

Years ago as I (Craig) was meditating on how the supernatural is released in our lives when we line our ways up with God's ways, the Lord reminded me of a physical principle which I had once studied in a college physics class. Everyone knows that the high-tension power lines that stretch across the land carry high voltage electricity. Electrical power from these lines can be accessed by physically connecting a conductive wire to these lines. However, few people know that electrical power can be induced in a conductor wire that is simply stretched parallel to an active electric line without the conductor wire's ever touching the line or being physically connected to it in any way. Because there is an electromagnetic field surrounding the power line, when another conductive wire is stretched parallel to a set of electric lines, it interfaces with this electromagnetic field and induces electric current to flow in the parallel wire. On the other hand, a conductor wire stretched perpendicular to the active electric line will not conduct any power at all. Electrical power line workers have been electrocuted when forgetting this vital principle.

Even as electrical power is induced across free air to a parallel conductor wire, so God's supernatural power and life can be induced in you when your ways are lined up parallel to His ways. In this analogy, God's ways are like the active power line, and your ways are like the nearby conductor wire. This is certainly true in the financial realm and applies to our handling of debt. When your ways are lined up with God's ways, you release His supernatural power in your finances. As a matter of fact, Solomon tells us in the book of Proverbs that "*When a man's ways please the Lord, He makes even his enemies to be at peace with him.*" (Proverbs 16:7 NKJV) Thus, if you have creditors who are enemies to you and are not at peace with you, you might consider checking your ways!

I (Earl), at the completion of a seminar in South Africa, was told of a man, who owed quite a large sum of money to a corporation. This man calculated his closed-circle or budget and determined that all he could offer the company monthly toward paying his debt was ten Rand (about $1.70 US) per month. He went to the corporation and told them that this was the amount that he had available to pay. Even though this was a very small amount, the corporation saw the integrity of his heart and agreed to receive his ten Rand per month. He faithfully paid this amount for a little over a year, when a representative of the corporation called him one day and advised him that the corporation had decided to release him from the debt. This man's faithfulness to step up to his debt and do what he could do resulted in God's moving on the hearts of his creditors to totally release and forgive him of that debt.

After changing the focus, it is now possible to calculate a closed circle or budget. Once you have a closed circle, you now know how much money is available monthly to apply toward paying debt. With this information, you can now pray about how to allocate the money available to pay creditors. Now is the time to make a list of every one of your creditors, including family members.

With this list of creditors and the total amount available monthly form your debt column of your budget, you can now pray and ask the Lord how much to allocate to each creditor monthly. It is important that you allocate something to each creditor monthly. Some people allocate all of their available money to just a couple of creditors while avoiding contact with the other ones. This again violates God's ways and leaves you in the position of being wicked toward those creditors you are avoiding. Therefore, you need to allocate something to every creditor.

You are now ready to step up to your debt with your creditors. You can now contact each of your creditors and firstly confess your wrongdoing in not honoring your word to pay them. Ask them to forgive you and let them know that you are serious about stepping up to your debt and doing what you can to repay them. Make your proposal of what you are reasonably able to pay each month and ask them for their agreement.

We have found that most times creditors will work with a debtor in whom they sense sincerity and integrity and a genuine concern to repay the debt. Many times they will cancel the interest or even reduce the amount of the debt. Most creditors are very willing to work with someone who is willing to step up to his/her debt and come with a repayment plan.

Once you secure the agreement of each of your creditors, make sure now that you do what you have agreed to do. Make sure that you meet the agreed-upon monthly payment. You are in the process of once again establishing trust, so it is very important that you fully honor your word.

In stepping up to your debt and securing the agreement of each of your creditors, you are no longer in violation of the rules in the world system. You can now expect your financial life to move from the natural into the supernatural. You have lined up your copper wire with God's overhead electric line. You can rise in faith and believe God to intervene on your behalf. Kingdom principles can be activated and put to work to provide multiplication of resources to you for rapid debt reduction. Once you've made agreement with your creditors, you've changed something in the spirit realm and you've untied God's hands so that the supernatural can begin to work on your behalf. You'll be amazed at how resource will begin to become available from unexpected sources. Many times we have seen people, who by natural calculation of available finances, would take ten to twenty years to retire their debt, be entirely debt free in eighteen months or two to three years. This is a result of God's supernatural support in their lives.

When you are in debt and have not stepped up to your debt, securing the agreement of your creditors, what happens when you spend money on discretionary items? For example, suppose you take your family on a vacation. In reality you are spending your creditors' money without their authorization. You are wicked, and furthermore, you are a thief. However, after you have stepped up to your debt and made agreement with your creditors, now each month when your monthly payment obligations are met you are now free to pray about how to use any overflow that God may bring to you. God may lead you to use overflow to accelerate the rate at which you retire your debt. However, if your agreed-upon monthly debt repayment obligations are met, you are not a thief if you use overflow for some other purpose as directed by the Lord. Even though you still owe money to your creditors, the agreement of monthly repayment is their authorization for you to use overflow money, not already allocated in your closed-circle budget as directed by the Lord.

So, for example if I take my wife out to dinner before I have stepped up to my debt, I have just spent my creditors' money without their authorization. After I have stepped up to my debt and met my monthly repayment terms with all my creditors, now if I take my wife out to dinner, I can do so without guilt and without being wicked. This is a very powerful principle that very few people in the body of Christ seem to understand.

Stepping up to your debt will remove the guilt and emotional paralysis. We have seen that tremendous guilt usually pressures families who have not yet stepped up to their debt. Suppose such a family takes a family vacation. Do they enjoy their vacation? Usually they do not, as a result of all the strife created by arguments over money. Perhaps the children see a water park and say, "Oh, Dad, there's a water park. Please let's go to the water park." What does Dad say? "No! It's too expensive!" Now the children are hurt and angry, and continue to nag their father about the water park. Why does the father say "no?" He says "no," because in his heart he is already feeling guilty about the money spent on the vacation. He's laboring under this weight of his debt, and his heart realizes that while trying to bless his family, he is actually spending someone else's money without their authorization. He may also use the words "We can't afford that!" Those words can set up in the child's emotions a poverty mentality, which will linger with that person into his/her adult life. A better response is to say, "your mother and I have made a choice to use our money in this manner or for these items rather than for that!"

Perhaps the wife says, "Honey, I've always wanted to go to that restaurant that overlooks the beach." "No! It's too expensive!" exclaims the husband. "We're going to the cheap restaurant." Does this family enjoy their vacation? Not at all! They come back in need of a vacation from their vacation. The stress and pressure of debt with which they have not properly dealt has spoiled any potential enjoyment they might have had.

Let's consider the aspect of giving money in offerings when you have not yet stepped up to your debt. Some Christians will try to give to get out of debt. When we give, we must make sure to give that which is ours, not that which belongs to someone else. It is wrong to reach into someone else's pocket, take money and give it. If we have not stepped up to our debt and we give, we are actually giving money that does not belong to us. It belongs to our creditors. Normally, giving in an offering would be deposited into our Treasures in Heaven account. However, we believe that if one has not stepped up to debt and has creditors who are owed, and with whom agreement has not been made, such giving is actually deposited into the Treasures in Heaven accounts of the creditors. It is available to the creditors rather than to the giver. In this case, we frequently hear the debtor/giver proclaim, "The Kingdom of God principle of sowing and reaping does not work. I gave, and my financial situation has become no better."

SUMMARY OF THE PRACTICAL STEPS IN DEALING WITH DEBT

1. Repent of wickedness if you have borrowed and not repaid.
2. Change your focus. Focus on what you do have and what you can do.
3. Calculate your closed-circle or budget.
4. Make a list of all of your creditors.
5. Allocate a portion of the money available in the debt column of your budget to each creditor.
6. Contact each creditor and make an offer of what you can pay each month and secure the creditor's agreement.
7. Pay each creditor the agreed-upon amount monthly.
8. Look for ways to give from your closed circle and from overflow in order to make deposits in your Heavenly Account.
9. Expect God to move supernaturally on your behalf providing closed-circle overflow for rapid debt reduction.

CHAPTER 8
INCREASING FRUITS OF
RIGHTEOUSNESS

Let us now return to the uses of money mentioned in Second Corinthians 9. We will turn our attention to the meaning of using money to increase fruits of righteousness. Most people have never understood the meaning of increasing fruits of righteousness. Let's think for a moment about the opposite, using money in deeds of unrighteousness. We have seen that the spirit of Mammon motivates people to use relationships to make money. Money is used particularly in unrighteousness when usury is charged to place people in bondage to debt. Money, in this case, is used to oppress and enslave people. These are deeds of unrighteousness. Unrighteousness is agreeing with Mammon against humanity. Righteousness, on the other hand, would be to use money to free people from debt or slavery. God, as opposed to Mammon, desires to motivate people to use money to build relationships. Thus, we can increase fruits of righteousness when we use money to build relationships and to free others from the influence of the Mammon spirit.

I (Earl) first received some understanding about using money to increase fruits of righteousness when I was returning from a teaching time in Hong Kong in 1984. On the plane I was pondering this use of money. The amplified Bible states "**... and increase the fruits of your righteousness [which manifests itself in active goodness, kindness and charity].**" My thoughts went to the word "righteousness." When it came to money, my mind was aware of examples of how money was used for deeds of unrighteousness. Enslavement of people with usury (exorbitant rate of interest) is a major problem in our society today. Mammon is referred to in Luke 16 as Mammon of unrighteousness.

As I meditated on these thoughts, I felt that the Lord said to turn this around and look for deeds of righteousness using money. I then began meditating on the question, "How do we get people free from the bondage of debt?" I recalled the numerous businessmen in the church whom I had encountered, telling me of money they had given to people in serious financial trouble, only to find that the money was mismanaged, and the recipient continued in financial distress. In most cases, money given without accountability is mismanaged. I have found that financial distress is usually not caused by lack of funds, but rather by lack of training, discipline and a wrong philosophy of money management. As I was thinking about how to free people from debt, solve the problem of lack of training and accountability when money is given to those in distress, the Lord brought to my remembrance the following scripture.

PROVERBS 22

7   *The rich rules over the poor, and the borrower is servant to the lender. (NKJV)*

I had always been aware that a borrower subjects himself/herself to a lender and naturally had always seen this as a very negative thing to be avoided. I certainly did not want to be servant to a lender, and rightly so! However, the thought then occurred to me that a borrower, being servant to a lender, is not necessarily a negative thing if the lender is benevolent toward the borrower, and is motivated to help free the borrower from debt.

What if money, accompanied by strong accountability, were to be made available to those ensnared with usury and the demands of the worldly lenders? This would be for the purpose of training and freeing them. Money could be lent at no interest, rather than given to people on the condition there is to be accountability. The loan would be made only if the debtor were willing to submit his/her financial accounting to the lender on a regular (monthly or weekly) basis. The lender would, in turn, commit to teach the debtor Biblical financial principles and help him/her establish a closed circle including repayment of the loan.

The debtor's income and expenditures would then be reviewed monthly and the plan for next month would be established. By the time the money was repaid, the debtor should be on a firm foundation of Biblical financial management and should be able to be a blessing to others. While on the plane, I continued to ponder this concept. I then sensed the Lord's placing the thought in my mind that when I returned home, there would be money given to me that exceeded my closed circle. This money was to be set aside for increasing fruits of my righteousness. With that thought tucked away in my mind, I turned to other matters.

Upon arriving home, sure enough, my wife informed me that we had received a check for a sizable amount of money from a person we had known for many years. Remembering what the Lord had put in my mind, I shared my thoughts with my wife, Dorothy, and we deposited the check in the bank, to at least get interest on it! We then waited for further direction from the Lord. About two weeks later, I received a call from a friend who had just recently married and was working for a company in our town. His voice sounded urgent and after the formalities, he revealed to me a serious debt problem regarding his American Express card. He had an amount due in 48 hours and he had exhausted every available means to secure the funds with which to pay the debt. I probed awhile longer to get the background of previous months' payments, only to find out that he had been borrowing from his MasterCard and Visa to make the payment on the American Express card. The two cards were now at their maximum, thus creating the present problem. He now had no available credit with his bank, since his line of credit there was also at its maximum.

Immediately, my mind went to the thoughts I had on the airplane concerning increasing my fruits of righteousness. With this in mind, I arranged a time to meet this couple and review their overall financial situation. I was amused to note that this couple's total indebtedness on the three cards plus four additional cards, was within fifteen dollars of the amount of the check Dorothy and I had received two weeks earlier.

I shared what the Lord had placed in my mind on the plane, and offered to implement the plan. They were excited over this plan, which would involve the removal of their credit cards, and the establishment of accountability to me over their finances. We would work together to establish a closed circle, and a review would take place monthly of expenses compared to budget. The Biblical principles of finance would be shared and implemented.

They withdrew to talk and pray about the plan together. A short while later they returned to the table where we had been sitting, and I could see that the wife had been crying. They were beginning to realize some of the consequences of submitting to this plan. As borrower, they were agreeing to subject their financial management to me, the lender. Her husband could no longer carry a wad of bills in his pocket, having no awareness or tracking of what was being spent. Her spending habits had to drastically change with the removal of the cards. Obtaining receipts and recording expenditures were all new, and somewhat scary to them.

I sensed the fear and shame that they would find themselves in at this point, and yet relief that somehow this Mammon driven journey really could come to an end. Agreement was reached, and I wrote checks for each of the credit cards, putting them in envelopes with the statements, to be mailed in the morning. We had one other point of business before we prayed together. Disposition of the credit cards! I placed them on a slightly greased metal cookie sheet, arranging them so they touched each other. I turned the oven to broil and placed the cookie sheet in the oven for 5 minutes. When I took them out of the oven, they had nicely melted together. Once they were cool, the fused cards made a wall hanging! The sign to be placed under the hanging was "Never Do This Again!"

In the next meeting with this couple, I worked with them to establish a closed circle, as we described in the last chapter, utilizing the *God's Managers* book to track income and expenses. It was easy to establish a monthly payment to repay the loan I had made to them. We simply substituted the money that they had been using to service the minimum monthly payments to the card companies to repay the Fruits of Righteousness Loan without interest. Tithing however was a different story. They had been "occasionally borrowing the tithe" to cover other expenses. However, with the cards retired, money was immediately available to restore the Lord's tithe.

Since this type of management was new to this couple, for the first three months, it was necessary to meet every two weeks for prayer and encouragement and to review the plan. We also spent significant time engaging in spiritual warfare against the Mammon spirit that kept them in fear and self-pity over their situation. I found that bringing discipline to their handling of money was a serious struggle.

As we continued to meet, I recognized that this couple's repentance over the mismanagement of money needed to go much deeper. At first, it was like finding a child with his hand in the cookie jar. The tears were not tears of repentance, but rather tears of remorse for being caught! It took some time for this couple to come to grips with their own wickedness in borrowing and not repaying.

Sometimes I have found that it is necessary initially to take total control of the debtor's bank accounts by using such measures as adding to the accounts two-signature signing authorities, the lender's and the debtor's. Debit cards must also be relinquished in order to bring discipline to the financial situation. (There are people who make their living managing people's finances in this manner. Most will not take clients unless they earn over $100,000 dollars a year!)

Fortunately in this case, although contemplated at times, this type of micromanagement was not necessary. Through prayer, teaching the Word of God on finances, and the development of new habits and attitudes toward money, this couple was on the journey to financial recovery. After a few setbacks, freedom was on the horizon. Becoming tithers in the true sense of the Word, having their closed circle in place, this couple began to experience some overflow. The rate of repayment that we had originally calculated to repay the loan would have required several years to retire the debt. However, as they were faithful in the natural realm, God began moving on their behalf, and a significant raise in salary allowed the Fruits of Righteousness loan to be repaid in only 18 months. What a time of rejoicing that day was! After that time, the circle was reviewed and some adjustments made. The money that had been used to retire the fruits of righteousness account could now be reassigned for Kingdom purposes.

This couple became strong financial supporters of missions and was able to bless many people.

Some years later, I (Earl) was giving a financial seminar in my church, using the materials shared in this book. When I taught the section on Increasing Your Fruits of Righteousness, I noticed a woman wiping her tears with a tissue. Following the seminar, this woman came to me to talk about this subject and asked if I would be willing to help her in a way similar to the way I had helped the young couple. It was then that the Lord dropped another idea into my mind. I approached my Pastor to discuss the idea of setting up an Increasing Fruits of Righteousness Account in the church. I would find people who would make money available from their overflow, which, as needed would be lent to qualified applicants without interest and then repaid over time. Our Pastor thought that this was a great idea. As I presented this plan to business people in our congregation, I found that there was no shortage of those who wanted to bless others in financial distress, as long as there was accountability.

In the implementation of this program, I became responsible to review the church member applicants, get approval from the church council, and then follow through with the financial counseling and accountability. Most of the business people felt that they did not have the time or ability to take people through the process; however, many had a desire to see others walk in financial freedom and were willing to make money available for that purpose. Many had felt burned by those who had asked for and received financial help in the past with no accountability. In the long run, the situation of the debtor had not changed and the giver/lender had felt used.

Many such people had become unwilling to give money, yet felt guilty in seeing need and being unwilling to help. Some had expected their money to be paid back, but had fallen into the trap of "pay me back when you can." Others had simply given money to people in need, but had an uncomfortable feeling wondering if it would do any good. Due to the screening and accountability, those who had overflow money that could be used in this manner received this program gladly.

How many people sit in the church pews each week and have great need of spiritual and practical help in finances? The state of personal finances is the last great taboo about which nobody talks. Consequently, we are often not really aware of the actual situation in the homes of those other Christians around us. This "Increasing Fruits of Righteousness" program has been implemented with much success in our local congregation for over three years at this point of writing. We would encourage you to consider talking to your local church leadership about implementing a similar strategy in your own local congregation. I am sure that this program is only one of many ways that God has in mind for money to be used to increase fruits of righteousness. The Gospel truly is the power of God unto salvation, of spirit, soul, body, relationships and finances. Praise God!

Several years ago the Lord taught me (Craig) about using money to increase fruits of righteousness through an experience I had with two businessmen. Paul and Roger (not their real names) had been involved in a particular business deal together. Paul was a very wealthy man, while Roger was always falling short of meeting his financial needs each month. Roger had gotten Paul involved in a particular business deal hoping that the success of this deal would eliminate his debt and solve his financial problems. Unfortunately, the deal had not worked, and Paul had lost quite a sum of money. Now all that was left was some residual stock that was in dispute between Paul and Roger. Since they could not bring resolution to their dispute, they asked me if I would help them to find a solution.

When we sat down together, I discovered that another factor in the dispute was the fact that Paul had conveyed to Roger personal loans of quite a large sum of money over the course of a couple of years. Because these men were personal friends, Roger would frequently ask Paul to lend to him whenever he was lacking money to meet his personal obligations. In our meeting, Paul brought up the fact that Roger had never paid him one dollar on his personal debt and just continued to ask for more loans every time he was short. Paul felt used and also that Roger had taken advantage of his friendship.

In our discussion, I introduced Roger to the concept of stepping up to his debt. He agreed that he would do this and would begin to pay $100 per month toward his debt. Paul then agreed that if Roger would at least do this, he was willing to split some of the residual stock with Roger. I thought that the dispute was resolved. However, three months later Roger called me alleging that Paul had not given him any of the stock and had not kept his word. Upon talking to Paul, I discovered that Roger had still not paid the first $100 on his personal debt. The two men agreed to meet me again the following Thursday.

Saturday night before the Thursday meeting I was having trouble sleeping. Jan, my wife, also could not sleep and went downstairs. I began thinking about this situation with Roger and Paul. As I was thinking about this, I heard the Lord say to me, "I want you to pay Roger's debt." At first I was surprised. My natural mind began to think about all the other things for which I could use that sum of money. I thought, "If we are to give it, wouldn't it make much more sense to give to missions, or to some of the poorer people in our church?" It didn't seem to make much sense to me to give a significant sum of money to a man who was already very wealthy, only to retire the debt of a man who had, through his own foolishness, gotten himself deeply in debt.

However, the Lord continued to speak to me that we were to pay Roger's debt. I then remembered Earl's experience about how he had learned to use money to increase fruits of righteousness. This was a little different situation, but the principle seemed to be the same— to use money to build relationship and perhaps free both men from the influence of the spirit of Mammon. About this time Jan returned to our bedroom. She had been downstairs praying. I asked if the Lord had spoken to her. She said that He had and she wanted to know if the Lord had said anything to me. I confirmed that He had and asked her, "What did He tell you?" She said, "No, you first!" So I said, "O.K." and shared with her what I believed the Lord had told me. She said, "I believe that's the Lord, and we're supposed to do that." I queried, "Why do you think so?" She replied, "Because when I was downstairs, the Lord told me that He was speaking to you upstairs and that when I came back it would be something sort of unusual but that it was God speaking to you and I should agree with it." We both felt that the Lord would use this action to impact the lives of both men and release them from the influence of the spirit of Mammon.

When the Thursday meeting came, I shared with both Paul and Roger that I felt that the spirit of Mammon was strongly influencing them both. It was influencing Roger to focus on obtaining money to meet his needs and influencing Paul to preserve the money that he felt many others were trying to take away from him. I then let them both know that the Lord had instructed me to pay Roger's debt. At first, they both thought that I was talking about something spiritual rather than material. However, when I produced the checkbook and asked for the exact payee and amount, the reality of my payment suddenly hit both of them. Both men were shocked, and I believe something broke in the spirit realm over both of their lives that day. Roger did humble himself before Paul and asked for his forgiveness for presuming upon Paul's generosity. The dispute over the stock was then easily settled. I believe that this act of giving broke the power of the spirit of Mammon in both men's lives and refocused their attention on God.

Within the next couple of months, I observed that Paul began to release significant sums of money into the Kingdom of God to various ministries and mission organizations. A few months later I called Roger to see how he was doing and discovered that his business for the first time in years was flourishing. I asked him what he was doing differently than before. He answered, "Nothing that I know of. I am doing the same thing that I have always done, but somehow it is now working." He also began giving into the Kingdom of God.

After this experience, I was able to see the wisdom of the Lord in having Jan and me use this money in this way. We could have given it to the poor or to missions, and it would have accomplished a purpose. However, by giving it to Paul to pay Roger's debt, the money was multiplied many times in the Kingdom as fruits of righteousness were increased in the lives of both of these men. When the spirit of Mammon was broken over both of their lives, financial resources were then released into the Kingdom of God through both of them at a much greater rate than before.

So we see that increasing fruits of righteousness is another legitimate scriptural use of money. Had Jan and I not had the money available in overflow, we could not have used it in this way to increase the fruits of righteousness in Roger's and Paul's lives.

GENEROSITY: LIBERALITY OR GIVING

Generosity is another legitimate, scriptural use of money. Generosity is simply giving to others as the Lord directs. This is not tithing or sowing and reaping. Apostle Paul instructs us about giving in 2 Corinthians, chapter 9.

2 CORINTHIANS 9

7   *Let each one [give] as he has made up his own mind and purposed in his heart, not reluctantly or sorrowfully or under compulsion, for God loves (that is, He takes pleasure in, prizes above other things, and is unwilling to abandon or to do without) a cheerful (joyous, prompt-to-do-it) giver— whose heart is in his giving. (Amplified)*

This verse captures the heart of generosity. First of all, we need to make up our minds that we will give as the Lord instructs us. Our purpose of heart is to bless others. There are people who feel reluctant and are under compulsion to give. Firstly we must ask the Lord if we are to give in a given situation, so that we cannot be manipulated to give by people or circumstances. If the Lord has said you are not to give in a particular situation, then as you pass up the opportunity, you can do so with confidence, knowing that you are acting in obedience to the Lord. In a church offering situation, your conscience is clear, and you don't have to pretend that you are putting something in the offering receptacle when you are not. If the Lord has instructed you to give, the second question is, "How much?" Giving in obedience to the Lord then makes a deposit in your Treasures in Heaven account where the deposit multiplies.

LUKE 6

38   *Give, and [gifts] will be given you, good measure, pressed down, shaken together and running over will they pour into*

[the pouch formed by] the bosom [of your robe and used as a bag]. For with the measure you deal out- that is, with the measure you use when you confer benefits on others— it will be measured back to you. (Amplified)

The purpose of our giving is to release blessing to others. We do not give to receive, but rather out of obedience to God and His Word. When we discussed Treasures in Heaven in chapter 4, we saw that our giving is the mechanism God uses for us to heap up Treasures in Heaven. It is His command to keep us free from heaping up treasures on earth and having our heart follow that treasure. Giving and receiving is also the primary principle governing Kingdom finances.

Generosity then is simply having money available to bless those around us. We must have financial resources available to be able to buy somebody lunch, to be able to purchase a tank of fuel for someone's car, or to be able to buy somebody a suit of clothes. Thus, I must have money available to be able to bless those around me.

Receiving is the other side of the giving coin. There are many people who have problems receiving. They love to be givers, but when someone tries to give to them, they refuse it. We need to learn to receive joyfully; otherwise, we cheat others out of the blessing of giving. An inability to receive is usually rooted in false humility, which is actually a form of pride. Many struggle with a feeling of needing to repay an equal or greater amount to the person who gave. This is pride and demonstrates a lack of understanding the concept of grace. One reason God may want us to receive is so that we can be a pass-through channel of blessing to someone else.

A specific category of giving is the giving of alms to the poor.

PROVERBS 19

17 He who has pity on the poor, lends to the Lord, and that which he has given He will repay to him. (Amplified)

There is a one-time return promised on this type of giving. Jesus came to preach the Gospel to the poor.

LUKE 4

18 The Spirit of the Lord [is] upon Me, because He has anointed Me [the Anointed One, the Messiah] to preach the good news (the Gospel) to the poor; He has sent Me to announce release to the captives, and recovery of sight to the blind; to send forth delivered those who are oppressed— who are downtrodden, bruised, crushed and broken down by calamity. (Amplified)

Notice that each thing that Jesus was called and anointed to do had a result that was opposite to the problem. Thus the Gospel, which is the power of God, is preached to the poor and thereby breaks the power of Mammon over the lives of people and sets them free to enter into God's provision of prosperity with a purpose for blessing.

Thus, let us review the five uses of money, which we have discovered in 2 Corinthians 9.

1. **Tithing**. This money is ten percent of our gross income. It already belongs to the Lord, and is to be set aside as holy to be given into the storehouse.

2. **Bread for Eating**. This is resource available for our personal consumption and must be managed through a closed circle budget.

3. **Sowing and Reaping**. This money comes from overflow and is invested in the Kingdom of God with a deliberate intention to reap a multiplied harvest.

4. **Increasing Fruits of Righteousness**. This money is allocated to build relationships, and to deliver others from debt and the spirit of Mammon.

5. **Generosity**. This money is available to be given to the poor or others as the Lord directs and as one has purposed in his/her heart.

207

CHAPTER 9
MULTIPLY GOD'S RESOURCES IN SOWING AND REAPING

JOHN 4:23-24

SPIRIT	TRUTH
Faith *Romans 10:17* Word	Faith *Luke 17:5-10* Obedience
GRACE	**BUILDING BLOCKS**
2 CORINTHIANS 9:8 *And God is able to make all grace (every favor and earthly blessing) come to you in abundance, so that you may always and under all circumstances and whatever the need, be self sufficient, possessing enough to require no aid or support and furnished in abundance for every good work and charitable donation. (Amplified)*	1. RECOGNIZE AND RENOUNCE THE SPIRIT OF MAMMON (Heart allegiance goes to God alone) 2. ESTABLISH SPARROW FAITH (God is my source) 3. ESTABLISH THE TITHE (Be a tither rather than just tithing) 4. BECOME GOD'S MANAGER (Become accountable to God for administration of present resources) 5. CLOSE THE CIRCLE (How much is enough?) 6. STEP UP TO YOUR DEBT (Acknowledge and properly deal with all debt) 7. **BECOME A FINANCIAL EUNUCH** (Manage the overflow for the Lord)

BECOMING A FINANCIAL EUNUCH

As we begin to talk about sowing and reaping, it is important to understand that this is the seventh foundational principle that is being presented. The reason we say this is that many Christians have tried to start with this principle without first establishing the other critical principles. They then are disappointed, claim that it doesn't work, and end up angry with God and Bible teachers. In our earlier discussion we mentioned that sowing and reaping are not the principle used to meet our basic needs. Sowing and reaping are primarily for the Kingdom of God. When we have the other five principles of Sparrow Faith, establishing the tithe, closing our circle, becoming a manager, and stepping up to our debt in place, we now qualify ourselves to become a financial eunuch through sowing and reaping for the expansion of the Kingdom.

You may ask, **"What is a financial eunuch?"** Let us first consider the role of a physical eunuch in the ancient east. A eunuch was a man who had been castrated and therefore, had no sexual desire. The role of the eunuch was primarily to serve with the king's harem. The harem was comprised of the most beautiful women in the land, who were dedicated to the king. What would happen if a man touched one of the women in the king's harem for himself sexually? He would, of course, lose his life. These women were dedicated to the king alone and were not to be touched by anyone else. To insure that this would never happen, only eunuchs were allowed to serve around the king's harem.

The primary role of the eunuch was to work with and prepare the bride for her king. He had no desire to take the bride for himself. He had been totally stripped of this desire through castration. **A financial eunuch, then, is someone whose primary role is to handle financial resources for the King.** He/she would never touch this resource for self, as this desire has already been dealt a deathblow through establishing the first six principles in life.

So a financial eunuch is a person who comes to the Lord applying for the job of managing and handling a fiduciary account on behalf of the Lord for the purpose of expanding the Kingdom of God. You can now see why establishing the tithe is so important, as it is the initial qualification for this position. Recognizing that the tithe is not yours, but rather that it is the Lord's and is your first opportunity to manage a small fiduciary account on behalf of the Lord is the initial qualification for becoming a financial eunuch. If you cannot even manage the Lord's tithe and keep it holy unto the Lord, why would the Lord trust you to manage a larger cash flow on His behalf?

What would happen if you try to become a financial eunuch and don't yet have the other principles settled in your life? If you try to become a financial eunuch but have not yet settled Sparrow Faith in your heart, you will be tempted to touch part of the Lord's fiduciary account to meet your own obligations, necessities and wants. You may also be tempted to store up the Lord's funds in your barn rather than release them into the Kingdom. If you have not established the tithe, then you have not yet qualified yourself to manage a small fiduciary account and have proven yourself unfaithful to manage a larger one.

If you have not yet made the paradigm shift from being an owner to being a manager, then you will think that funds that are the Lord's are yours and will prove unfaithful to manage them on behalf of the Lord. You will touch them for yourself. If you have not yet closed your circle, then you will not even be able to distinguish the difference between that which is to be used for your obligations, necessities, and wants and that, which is the Lord's for the Kingdom. If you have not yet stepped up to your debt, then you will be sowing into the Treasures in Heaven accounts of your creditors.

Once you have these first six principles in place you are now ready to become a financial eunuch and multiply funds for the Kingdom through sowing and reaping. Your desire to touch these funds for yourself is gone, and you are now qualified to be a manager of funds on behalf of the Lord.

LIVING ON THE THIRD RIVER

Have you ever thought about funding Kingdom work from God's perspective? God has an infinite supply of resource. However, we usually see that churches and ministries doing Kingdom work have a very limited and usually scarce supply of resource. Why? Does

God not want to supply? No, this is not the problem. How does resource get from God's supply into the hands of the end-user ministries? This happens primarily through people. Each Christian is like a pipeline through which God desires to flow financial resource into the Kingdom. However, many of the pipelines are extremely clogged and leaky. Most of what God puts down the pipe never makes it out the other end. If Sparrow Faith is not established, fear causes most of the resource to be collected in the pipeline. If there is massive debt, then much of the resource is siphoned out of the pipeline in the form of interest. If the circle is not closed, then most of the resource is consumed on making a bigger, better and more comfortable pipe. We believe that this must be very frustrating for the Lord.

While teaching in Africa once, the Lord gave me (Craig) a picture depicting the management of financial resource. I saw a huge snowfield in the mountains with virtually an infinite supply of water. There were three rivers emanating from this snowfield. On the first river, lives a man whose experience of life is that he never quite has enough water. Life experiences taught him that. So, what does he do with the water coming down the river? He builds a dam in that river, and collects all the water that he possibly can in a lake behind his dam. This man's view of water includes only that which is available to him in his lake. Therefore, he must conserve water, and he must be very careful, because there's barely ever enough coming down for him.

Now, here's the second river that flows down from the snowfield. The man who lives along this river has life experience that tells him there's usually plenty of water for him, so there is no need to build a dam in the river. He decides to let the water just flow naturally, to use what he needs and let the rest flow on down the river for others who live downstream to use. This man perceives that there is plenty of water in the river to meet his needs and plenty of water for the people who live downstream. So, he lives his life that way on the river, taking what he needs out of the river, and letting the rest flow on downstream.

Then there is a third river and a man who also lives along this river. His experience of life is that there is so much water up there in that snowfield that one could never use all the water coming down the river. As a result of this understanding, this man has begun digging canals to outlying areas to help water the fields of others who don't live near a river. Each year he digs a few new canals out to his neighbors, who need water. In the next year, this man has a plan for another 3 canals. Then the following year, he's hoping to dig 5 new canals that can go out even further from this river. It seems like no matter how many canals he digs, there's just more water that keeps coming down the river, so he just keeps digging canals. As a matter of fact, this man is thinking all the time how he can hire some more men with more bulldozers to help dig canals faster to get water out to all these other farms that are far from the river. This man's experience of life is that he just can't use up all that water.

Now suppose that you are the person in the snowfield who decides how much water to release into each river. Which river are you going to tend to put most of the water down? Probably river number 3. How much are you going to release into river number 1? You will probably put enough down this river to meet the need of that man who lives down there because you love him, and you want him to be taken care of. However, there's no use for that water making a large lake on his property. It just becomes stagnant, like a Dead Sea. So, you put just enough water down there for the man to use it, and that's all you're going to put in that one.

How much water would you put in the second river? You would probably send only enough water to meet the need of the people who live along that river. However, there is no point in sending huge quantities of water down this river, as it will be improperly used. The majority of water will of course be sent down the third river, so that it will be utilized to bring the most benefit to the greatest number of people.

I have found that many times non-Christians have a better sense of living along the third river than do Christians. I have found unbelievers who have learned to live with a closed circle and are really already living along the third river, while their Christian neighbors are still living along the first or second rivers believing God for "the wealth of the wicked to be transferred to the righteous." I believe that from God's perspective it may be easier to bring the unbeliever living on the third river into the Kingdom than to get the Christian living on the first or second river to shift paradigms to live on the third river. This may surprise many Christians as God builds His Kingdom in this new millennium. The sons of darkness sometimes exercise more wisdom than the sons of light.

In reality, whatever water is flowing down your river right now is probably about the amount that God finds you faithful to manage. If you desire to manage a greater portion of God's resources as a steward, this will require that you allow God to change you significantly on the inside. People who are accustomed to managing $100 million per year think very differently from people accustomed to managing $100 thousand per year. Again, I believe that it would be much easier for the Lord to bring into His Kingdom someone accustomed to managing $100 million per year as a steward and flow such a cash flow of His resource through him/her into the Kingdom, than to try to teach a person who is already in the Kingdom, who is accustomed to dealing with $100 thousand per year, or less, how to become a steward over $100 million per year.

Thus, in order to qualify ourselves to be managers over more of the Lord's resource, we must learn to be faithful over what we have been given to manage now. Then we can allow the Lord to bring about necessary change in our thinking and perceptions of life to be able to understand how to manage greater amounts of resources in His Kingdom. When I have learned how to live along the third river with the resources that I now have, I qualify myself to receive more of God's resources to channel into His Kingdom. The faster I can learn to build canals and channel resources into the Kingdom, the faster I qualify myself to handle more resources. I believe that the Lord is simply looking for people with a credible track record, not people who are full of only good intentions, of "what they will do when they have such and such resources." For many of us this is a major paradigm shift that will have to take place now in order to qualify us for the plan God has for us for the future.

SOWING AND REAPING: THE CORRECT PURPOSE

The concept of sowing and reaping is a foundational principle of the Kingdom of God.

MARK 4

26 *And He said, The Kingdom of God is like a man who scatters seed upon the ground,*

27 *Then continues sleeping and rising night and day while the seed sprouts and grows and increases, he knows not how*

28 *The earth produces [acting] by itself, first the blade, then the ear, then the full grain in the ear.*

29 *But when the grain is ripe and permits, immediately he sends forth [the reapers] and puts in the sickle, because the harvest stands ready. (Amplified)*

The principle of sowing and reaping is also expressed in Second Corinthians 9.

2 CORINTHIANS 9

6 *[Remember] this: he who sows sparingly and grudgingly will also reap sparingly and grudgingly, and he who sows generously and that blessings may come to someone, will also reap generously and with blessings. (Amplified)*

The principle of sowing and reaping operates on a different basis from generosity or giving. Neither giving nor generosity has a purposeful expectation. The primary purpose of giving and generosity is simply to bless others. However, when we enter into sowing and reaping, there is a purposeful intent to reap when we sow. Sowing and reaping can be likened to farming. There is a very purposeful intent to farming. A farmer does not just scatter his seed hither and yon with no attention paid to how, when, where, preparation of soil, etc. No! When a farmer receives seed to sow, he enters into a very intentional process that will maximize the harvest from his seed. He first chooses his field and prepares the ground by plowing. He then plants his seed, fertilizes, irrigates and adds nutrient to his growing crop as necessary.

The farmer is not surprised when small green shoots come up through the ground and begin to grow. He is standing in expectation of a harvest. The farmer will protect his seed, by driving the birds away and watching for anything that would affect his harvest. In the course of this process, he sleeps and rises, sleeps and rises; the seed sprouts and grows, and he knows not how. The farmer is not responsible for the growth. He cannot cause the seed to grow. This is God's job. When harvest time has arrived; he will labor and bring the harvest in. Harvest time then requires work. The sowing and reaping system thus becomes a full-time occupation. In certain climates in the world one can at the same time be sowing in one field and reaping in another with differing types of crops. A good farmer will not sow more than he has time to watch over and ultimately reap.

How does a farmer use his harvest? He will not use all the harvest for seeding once again. The farmer will tithe from the harvest and set aside seed for sowing again. Then he will use some of the seed for converting into money for buying and selling, meeting his own necessities, and having a portion to give to others. Some of the seed will be set aside for emergency purposes. Now as we consider the principle of using money for multiplication of resources for sowing, God will place overflow in our hands for specific purposes.

Let's consider the Kingdom financial model. God is our source, and He provides money that can be given as He directs us. The money that is given blesses and is accounted for by making a deposit in our Treasures in Heaven account. Jesus oversees the account and provides an increase factor over the account so that there is more in the account than what has been deposited. Now for us as tithers, the window of heaven is opened and the blessing flows from our Heavenly account to meet our closed-circle or budget.

The portion of that circle that involves basic necessities (clothing, food and shelter), God promises to meet on the basis of Sparrow Faith, simply because He loves us. However, His desire is first to fill and then to overflow our closed circle so we can be a blessing in the world and carry out His plans and purpose through us in the world. After our obligations, necessities and wants that are in the circle have been met, we have overflow or a multiplication of seed for sowing. This overflow is to be directed by God and invested where He wants it to go. Not the entire overflow is necessarily seed. It could be that He wants you to give a portion over and above the giving from your closed circle. Some will be held in riches in the world system, ready for the Master's use, just as the colt was available for Jesus (Mark 11:2-6). This would mean that you must be able to have access to the riches that you have invested in the world system. Some of this overflow, the Lord may also want to be moved into wealth.

DEUTERONOMY 8

17 *And beware lest you say in your [mind and] heart, My power and the might of my hand have gotten me this wealth.*

18 *But you shall (earnestly) remember the Lord your God; for it is He Who gives you the power to get wealth, that He may establish His covenant which He swore to your fathers, as at this day. (Amplified)*

God will provide overflow to your closed circle for the purposes of wealth creation. Now you remember that wealth is defined biblically as land, houses, cattle and flocks (means of reproduction), gold and silver in the form of bullion or jewelry (asset formation for financial backing) and man and maid servants (intellectual creativity). God is releasing overflow for the purposes of His Kingdom and its expansion in the earth. The world system has its own version of the sowing and reaping principle. It is called investment. A person may take some money that is above his/her obligations and needs and call a financial planner to have him/her invest this money in the world system markets. If he prospers, there will be some amount of percentage increase. However, this type of investment only builds structures in the world system. It may provide capital for industry or high-rise buildings for offices and the world system institutions. Now none of this need be morally wrong; however, if God wants it for His Kingdom, then we, as Christians, may have it in the wrong kingdom.

The Kingdom of God has its own system of investment. It is called the principle of sowing and reaping. We have seen in the Word that when the Word of God was sown as seed into a person's life, there are many factors that could potentially destroy or hinder the multiplication of this seed.

MARK 4

14 The sower sows the Word.

15 The ones along the path are those who have the Word sown [in their hearts], but when they hear, Satan comes at once and (by force) takes away the message which is sown in them.

16 And in the same way the ones sown upon stony ground are those who, when they hear the Word, at once receive and accept and welcome it with joy;

17 And they have no real root in themselves, and so they endure for a little while, then when trouble or persecution arises on account of the Word, they immediately are offended— become displeased, indignant, resentful; and they stumble and fall away.

18 And the ones sown among the thorns are others who hear the Word,

19 Then the cares and anxieties of the world, and distractions of the age, and the pleasure and delight and false glamour and deceitfulness of riches, and the craving and passionate desire for other things creep in and choke and suffocate the Word, and it becomes fruitless.

20 And those that were sown on the good (well adapted) soil are the ones who hear the Word, and receive and accept and welcome it, and bear fruit, some thirty times as much as was sown, some sixty times as much, and some [even] a hundred times as much. (Amplified)

I (Earl) saw this principle at work in a very practical way a number of years ago. The Lord had financially blessed Dorothy and me. We were tithers and had given much over the years. However, we had never experienced a multiplication of money returned. As we thought about this, we discovered that the reason for this was that we had never purposefully sown seed! We had tithed, given in generosity to others, but had never deliberately sown. As we prayed about this concept from the Word, we felt led to test the principle. We knew a fellow who was involved in a Christian ministry. I contacted him and shared with him what we were seeing in the Word pertaining to multiplication. We had a sum of money that was in the overflow category from our closed circle that we knew was to be used as seed. We were led to sow this sum into the Kingdom by meeting with my friend and placing it in his hand and telling him that this was not a gift or a giving, but rather it was seed that I was believing would multiply back to us ten-fold. We knew that we needed to watch over our seed, as there were many things that could destroy its multiplied return.

We would pray for our friend and the ministry, and conduct spiritual warfare as the Lord prompted us. He would do the same for us. As the seed was sown, we slept and rose and where the increase was coming from, we did not know! Some may ask, "How long does it take to realize the harvest?" In the natural realm, it depends on the type of seed. In the realm of the spirit, harvest comes when God is finished accomplishing His purpose. God could multiply it back instantaneously as He did when Jesus fed the five thousand. Jesus received the five loaves and two small fish, and praising God, He gave thanks, broke the loaves and kept on giving them to the disciples to set before the people. He did the same with the fish. At the end, there were twelve hand baskets full of the broken pieces (Mark 6:41 & 43). God is often times more interested in the prayer and spiritual warfare that are being offered than multiplying money back to us. He is simply using money as a tool for His purposes. I believe that it comes back multiplied when God has accomplished His desire through our "watching over the seed" by prayer and spiritual warfare.

During the next six weeks my friend and I were communicating and sharing what God was doing in our lives and watching for the harvest. One evening at our home after a Bible study with a group of people, a fellow came to me with an envelope containing a check. He stated that he had been reasoning with God for several days over giving me this money. He knew I worked for the IBM Corporation and with my salary I surely did not need this money! However, in obedience to what God had impressed on his heart, he was handing this money to me. When I opened the envelope, to my amazement, the check was written for an amount exactly ten times what I had sown! I was so excited that I did not know whether to laugh or cry.

That experience established something in my heart. It settled the issue about God's system of sowing and reaping. Now the question is where does this increase go? My closed circle budget was already met, and this seed was out of overflow that God had provided as a multiplication of seed for sowing. The use of the harvest needs to be directed by the Lord. It may be that the Lord will direct you to give a portion, which results in a deposit in your Treasures in Heaven account. Some could be seed for the next sowing when directed by the Lord. Some may be held in 'escrow' for future use as the Lord shows you. This may be in some form of riches that is money working for you until the 'Master has need of it.' However, when Kingdom principles provide the increase, the harvest is for Kingdom use in some manner.

There are **six principles** that I (Earl) have learned from experiences in sowing and reaping that I would like now to share with you.

1. Moneys for this multiplication program come primarily from overflow to your closed circle. I counsel with people who have tried to take seed from an OPEN circle hoping to get multiplication to meet their needs and wants. When it does not work, they blame God or someone's teaching. God can and has moved sovereignly in people's finances and provided one-time miracles. However, He expects us to operate in His principles so His blessing flows continuously. Get your financial house in order.

2. There is a difference between giving and sowing. Sowing is work, while giving is just a fun thing to do, as we are directed by the Lord. It is the difference between farming and just throwing some seed out the window and not following its growth to know when to harvest. Thus, you

need to ask God when He prompts you to be involved financially, "Lord, is this giving or sowing?"

3. In believing God for the multiplication, some ask why not believe for 100-fold return on everything? First of all, it is a faith issue. Do you have 100-fold faith? Why did I believe for a ten-fold return? That was the level of my faith. I have learned that the larger the number the more the work! How much time are you willing to allocate to prayer and spiritual warfare? The increase is coming out of the world system. The money is in that system. God is not a counterfeiter! The Mammon spirit is against you and will try to withhold the return, especially when he knows you are going to use this money for Kingdom purposes. Where you sow the money is important. Not all ground in Kingdom ministries is the same. Some ground is not able to produce a 100-fold return. Ask God where you are to sow. Then ask the Lord for optimum yield from that seed.

4. You must order your financial house. In other words, get your circle closed, step up to your debt, and eliminate consumer debt. Be a tither and a giver, posturing yourself for an exciting spiritual venture into Kingdom finances.

5. Never sow more than you can look after through prayer and spiritual warfare. I believe there is much seed that has been sown and forgotten by the sower. A farmer knows what has been sown and waits prepared to harvest when the crop stands ready (Galatians 6).

6. Do not lose heart and grow weary in acting nobly and doing right, for in due time and at the appointed season you shall reap, if you do not loosen and relax your courage and faint. (Galatians 6:9) Reaping or harvesting involves work! This verse applies to all types of sowing and reaping, but it includes finances as well.

I (Earl) remember a time when a group of YWAM staff had received an offering to sow financially into a boat ministry in the Micronesian islands. They continued to pray and conduct spiritual warfare for the release of a boat for the purpose of ministry. Months went by and they saw no release of the harvest (boat). Finally, after the boat was released and the ministry started, the question was asked, "Why did it take so long?" God could have released the boat immediately. However, the prayer support and intercession would not have continued as they would have been on to the next project without properly preparing for harvest. The preparation in this case required workers to properly maintain the boat and workers to do the ministry as well as a cash flow to support the operations. God knows the necessary releases in the spirit realm that only prayer can provide before the harvest is realized. It is critical to understand that you must watch over your seed. There is work involved.

MARK 4

23 *If any man has ears to hear, let him be listening, and perceive and comprehend.*

24 *And He said to them, 'Be careful what you are hearing. The measure [of thought and study] you give [to the truth you hear] will be the measure [of virtue and knowledge] that comes back to you, and more [besides] will be given to you who hear.*

25 *For to him who has will more be given, and from him who has nothing, even what he has will be taken away (by force),' (Amplified)*

I am glad that I did not have to write this scripture. I am only reporting to you the scriptural content! Below is Mark 4:19 with Earl's paraphrase of the Amplified version. *Don't let the cares and anxieties of the world, the pressure that the world wants to put on you over finances, and the distractions of this present age and the pleasure and delight and false glamour and the deceitfulness of riches (money working for you) and the craving and passionate desire for other things, (in other words get your circle closed), creep in and choke the Word about finances so it becomes fruitless, and will not provide for you. Then you will be consigned to the world system and only what it can provide.*

I have also discovered that there can be a disproportionate harvest returned for the seed sown. God is God, and He wants us to seek Him, not the harvest. He is the Lord of the harvest. There can also be a harvest in other than like kind. In the natural, you sow corn and reap corn; you sow wheat and reap wheat.

1 CORINTHIANS 9

11   If we have sown [the seed of] spiritual good among you, [is it too] much if we reap from your material benefits? (Amplified)

This is a harvest in other than like kind. How do you measure this harvest? You cannot do it, so there can be a disproportionate harvest. This type of harvest can also occur in a like kind situation, where the 100% return is many times greater, and God provides an optimal return. He is God, and He is not limited to a specified number increase.

Jesus taught about the requirement for multiplication in the Kingdom of God in the following two parables. In Matthew 25:14-29, the parable addresses a group of servants whose master gave talents to them in different amounts.

MATTHEW 25

14   For it is as a man who was about to take a long journey, and he called his servants together and entrusted them with his property.

(The master apparently converted wealth (property) into money, in order to have it work for him.)

MATTHEW 25

15   To one he gave five talents [probably about $5,000], to another two and to another one; to each in proportion to his own personal ability. Then he departed and left the country. (Amplified)

Notice that the talents <u>were given</u> to them. They <u>did not earn or work</u> for them. Some have thought that a talent is an ability or gift, since the same word is used this way in English. However, it is clear from the parable that the talent spoken of here is a unit of money. The servant in verse 27 clearly stated this.

MATTHEW 25

27 *Then you should have <u>invested my money</u> with the bankers, and at my coming I could have received what was my own with interest. (Amplified)*

So we see that receiving interest from the world system is the minimum requirement for the usage of money in the Kingdom. The money was traded or made to work for them, such that the first two servants multiplied it by a factor of two by the time there was a call for accountability. The master then returned and commented on the work that had been done with his money.

MATTHEW 25

20 *And he who had received the five talents came and brought him five more, saying, Master, you entrusted to me five talents; see, here I have gained five talents more.*

21 *His master said to him, Well done, you upright (honorable, admirable] and faithful servant! You have been faithful and trustworthy over a little; I will put you in charge of much, Enter into and share the joy –the delight, the blessedness— which your master [enjoys]. (Amplified)*

The master said, "Well done." The Moffit translation translates this as, **"Capital."** We feel that this expresses the heart of what has been accomplished. Riches were being formed through money that was working for the servant. God wants to give us overflow and have it start to work for us. Notice the master's reward of additional responsibility!

The servant that did not accomplish anything with the talent was called wicked, lazy and idle (verse 26).

MATTHEW 25

28 *So take the talent away from him, and give it to the one who has the ten talents.*

29 *For to every one who has will more be given, and he will be furnished richly so that he will have abundance. (Amplified)*

This comment by Jesus is familiar, as we have seen the principle demonstrated in Mark 4:24, 25. When dealing with finance, fear often grips one's heart. In such case, there can be excuses and unjust accusations such as this servant brought against the master as being a harsh and hard man who reaps where he did not sow. One of the principles seen in the parable is that when wealth is converted to money and given or entrusted to someone, there is a responsibility to put it to work with a multiplying factor.

In a second parable recorded in Luke 19, we find another group of people who are referred to as bondservants. This word bondservant is a different Greek word from the word translated, servant, found in Matthew 25. The term "bondservant" refers to a person who had been a slave and has been given his freedom. He then chooses to return to his master and serve him out of his own free will. This term would represent you and me as Christians. Jesus died for us to set us free from sin and the domination of the world system. We now are free to love and serve Him out of our own free will. In the parable, a certain nobleman was going to a distant country.

LUKE 19

13 *Calling ten of his [own] bond servants, he gave then ten minas [each equal to about one hundred days' wages or nearly twenty dollars], and said to them, Buy and sell with these while I go and return. (Amplified)*

The mina again is a unit of money as we see it in verse 24. Each bond servant was given the same amount of money. When the nobleman returned he called for accountability.

LUKE 19

16 *The first one came before him and he said, Lord, your mina has made ten [additional] minas.*

17 *And he said to him, Well done, excellent bond servant! Because you have been faithful and trustworthy in a very little, you shall have authority over ten cities. (Amplified)*

When they were no longer simply servants, but rather bond-servants, notice the increase in the multiplication factor that was available to them. The nobleman's response was now the granting of authority, not just responsibility. The money was referred to as a "very little thing." In Luke 16:10, Jesus said,

LUKE 16

10 *He who is faithful in a very little [thing], is faithful also in much; and he who is dishonest and unjust in a very little [thing], is dishonest and unjust also in much. (Amplified)*

Luke 16 is talking about money also as a little (thing). The world system sees money as a big thing. The Mammon spirit wants it to be a big deal in our lives. We must not be tempted by its so-called power; neither can we develop an "easy come, easy go" attitude. Jesus wants us to learn faithfulness and stewardship in our handling of money, and He leaves us in the world to learn these character principles. We do not know how this money multiplied for the bond-servants. However, God has creative ideas for us that will provide increase if we listen to Him and obey His voice.

CONCLUSION

2 CORINTHIANS 9

8 *And God is able to make all grace (every favor and earthly blessing) come to you in abundance, so that you may always and under all circumstances and whatever the need, be self-sufficient— possessing enough to require no aid or support and furnished in abundance for every good work and charitable donation. (Amplified)*

Is that your desire? God is able (but it is not automatic) to make all grace come to you in abundance. In conclusion, we would like to review here the seven basic principles from the Word of God, which will help you in dealing with your finances so that 2 Corinthians 9:8 will be effective in your life.

JOHN 4:23-24

SPIRIT	TRUTH
Faith *Romans 10:17* **Word**	**Faith** *Luke 17:5-10* **Obedience**
GRACE	**BUILDING BLOCKS**
2 Corinthians 9:8 *"And God is able to make all grace (every favor and earthly blessing) come to you in abundance, so that you may always and under all circumstances and whatever the need, be self sufficient, possessing enough to require no aid or support and furnished in abundance for every good work and charitable donation."*	1. **RECOGNIZE AND RENOUNCE THE SPIRIT OF MAMMON** (Heart allegiance goes to God alone) 2. **ESTABLISH SPARROW FAITH** (God is my source) 3. **ESTABLISH THE TITHE** (Be a tither rather than just tithing) 4. **BECOME GOD'S MANAGER** (Become accountable to God for administration of present resources) 5. **CLOSE THE CIRCLE** (How much is enough?) 6. **STEP UP TO YOUR DEBT** (Acknowledge and properly deal with all debt) 7. **BECOME A FINANCIAL EUNUCH** (Manage the overflow for the Lord)

Money is to be a servant to the wisdom of God. It takes God's wisdom to keep money from destroying us. Money is like a beach ball upon which one stands in a swimming pool. It is continually trying to escape to the surface, and constant attention must be paid to it to keep it in its place. Money is like poison; it is a blessing only when used properly and with great care. May God continue to give you His wisdom in properly managing the WEALTH, RICHES AND MONEY He has made available to you!

APPENDIX 1

The book, "*God's Managers, A Budget Guide and Daily Financial Record Book for Christians*", by Ray and Lillian Bair, is available through your local Christian bookstore or it can be ordered from the publisher, Herald Press, Scottdale, PA. U.S.A. 15683. The ISBN number is 0-8361-3406-0.

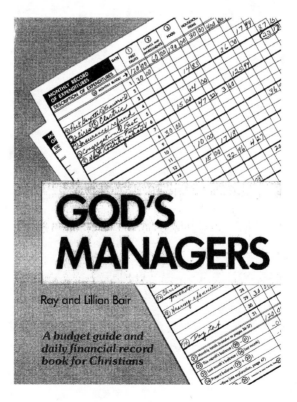

The following pages from the book, which are used as illustrations for the text in the Chapter 6, are used with permission of the publisher.

MONTHLY INCOME RECORD

JANUARY			FEBRUARY			MARCH			APRIL		
DATE	SOURCE	AMOUNT	DATE	SOURCE	AMOUNT	DATE	SOURCE	AMOUNT	DATE	SOURCE	AMOUNT
TOTAL INCOME FOR MONTH			TOTAL INCOME FOR MONTH			TOTAL INCOME FOR MONTH			TOTAL INCOME FOR MONTH		

MAY			JUNE			JULY			AUGUST		
DATE	SOURCE	AMOUNT	DATE	SOURCE	AMOUNT	DATE	SOURCE	AMOUNT	DATE	SOURCE	AMOUNT
TOTAL INCOME FOR MONTH			TOTAL INCOME FOR MONTH			TOTAL INCOME FOR MONTH			TOTAL INCOME FOR MONTH		

SEPTEMBER			OCTOBER			NOVEMBER			DECEMBER		
DATE	SOURCE	AMOUNT	DATE	SOURCE	AMOUNT	DATE	SOURCE	AMOUNT	DATE	SOURCE	AMOUNT
TOTAL INCOME FOR MONTH			TOTAL INCOME FOR MONTH			TOTAL INCOME FOR MONTH			TOTAL INCOME FOR MONTH		

10

God's Managers, a budget guide and daily financial record book for Christians, by Ray and Lillian Bair

MONTHLY RECORD OF EXPENDITURES DESCRIPTION OF EXPENDITURES	DATE	① FIRST FRUITS		② SAVINGS/ INVESTMENTS		③ FOOD		④ HOUSEHOLD ITEMS		⑤ HOUSING		⑥ CLOTHING		⑦ TRANSPOR TATION		⑧ EDUCATION	
⑳ MONTHLY BUDGET →																	
	1																
	2																
	3																
	4																
	5																
	6																
	7																
	8																
	9																
	10																
	11																
	12																
	13																
	14																
	15																
	16																
	17																
	18																
	19																
	20																
	21																
	22																
	23																
	24																
	25																
	26																
	27																
	28																
	29																
	30																
	31																
㉑ Monthly totals (transfer to pages 36-37)																	
㉒ This month's balance (⑳ − ㉑)																	
㉓ Last month's balance (㉖ last month)																	
㉔ Present balance (㉒ + ㉓)																	
㉕ Overflow (see explanation, page 47)																	
㉖ Balance (㉔ − ㉕) transfer to next month line ㉓																	

12   JANUARY

God's Managers, a budget guide and daily financial record book for Christians, by Ray and Lillian Bair

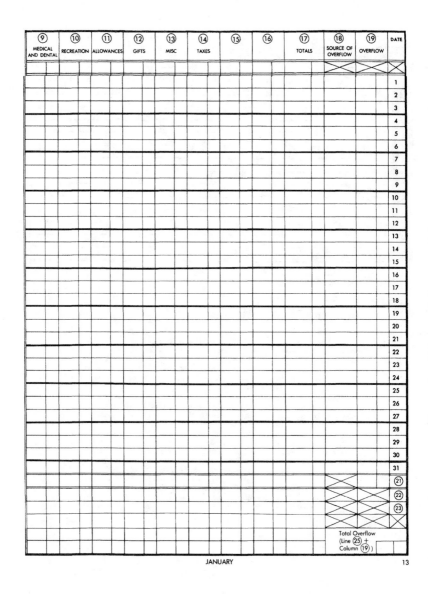

⑨ MEDICAL AND DENTAL	⑩ RECREATION	⑪ ALLOWANCES	⑫ GIFTS	⑬ MISC	⑭ TAXES	⑮	⑯	⑰ TOTALS	⑱ SOURCE OF OVERFLOW	⑲ OVERFLOW	DATE
											1
											2
											3
											4
											5
											6
											7
											8
											9
											10
											11
											12
											13
											14
											15
											16
											17
											18
											19
											20
											21
											22
											23
											24
											25
											26
											27
											28
											29
											30
											31
											㉑
											㉒
											㉓
										Total Overflow (Line ㉕ + Column ⑲)		

JANUARY

13

God's Managers, a budget guide and daily financial record book for Christians, by Ray and Lillian Bair

MONTHLY RECORD OF EXPENDITURES DESCRIPTION OF EXPENDITURES	DATE	① FIRST FRUITS	② SAVINGS/ INVESTMENTS	③ FOOD	④ HOUSEHOLD ITEMS	⑤ HOUSING	⑥ CLOTHING	⑦ TRANSPOR- TATION	⑧ EDUCATION
⑳ MONTHLY BUDGET →									
JANUARY (Line ㉑) 1									
FEBRUARY " "									
MARCH " "									
APRIL " "									
MAY " "									
JUNE " "									
JULY " "									
AUGUST " "									
SEPTEMBER " "									
OCTOBER " "									
NOVEMBER " "									
DECEMBER " "									
㉗ Total expenditures for year									
㉘ Budget total this year (⑳ X 12)									

(Continued from page 9)
PART TWO

Creating a Monthly Budget

We now come to the most important tool the good manager uses in performing the task well—the budget Keeping records without developing a budget is like going on a trip, keeping a written record of all the towns visited, but never deciding ahead of time where one wants to go, nor why Some people might enjoy that kind of travel for a while, but over the long term they would not experience the anticipation and joy that planning ahead can bring Nor would their traveling likely reflect the deeper long-range purposes of their lives as it would if they did careful planning beforehand

While this process may seem difficult, remember that the hard work is mostly in the first budget year In that first year you are creating the basic pattern Only minor adjustments and simple changes will likely be needed in the years afterward

The following procedure assumes the creation of a budget with 12 months' records at hand If you wish to work at a budget sooner than that you can use the following steps but will need to make the adjustments appropriate for the number of months' records you possess

So with your twelve-month record of expenditures before you, create a monthly budget by taking each column separately and working through the following process:

Step 1 Make certain all figures in line ㉑ from each of the 12 months' records have been transferred to the above ledger spaces on these two pages (36 and 37) You now have before you your full financial picture for the past year You now know where all your money has gone!

God's Managers, a budget guide and daily financial record book for Christians, by Ray and Lillian Bair

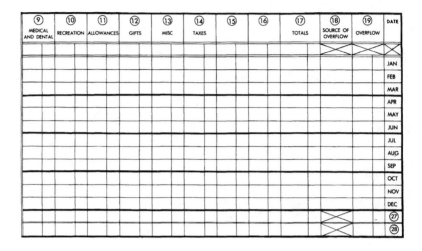

⑨ MEDICAL AND DENTAL	⑩ RECREATION	⑪ ALLOWANCES	⑫ GIFTS	⑬ MISC	⑭ TAXES	⑮	⑯	⑰ TOTALS	⑱ SOURCE OF OVERFLOW	⑲ OVERFLOW	DATE
											JAN
											FEB
											MAR
											APR
											MAY
											JUN
											JUL
											AUG
											SEP
											OCT
											NOV
											DEC
											㉗
											㉘

Step 2 Add the figures in each column above from top to bottom and place the totals on line ㉗ You now have on line ㉗ your total financial activity in each of the categories for the past year

Step 3 Review all the major expenditures of the past year Are there any (such as replacing your car, a major remodeling of the house, etc) that would not be "normal" annual expenses? Were they paid for by cash (that is, not set up on payments by taking out a loan)? If so, then you will want to subtract the total paid in cash from your annual total in that category If that major expense would be something that usually occurs, say, every five years, you would then divide that expense by five and add the resulting figure back into the total for the year in that category

To illustrate: Let's suppose that during the past year you traded cars and the difference paid was $3,000 cash Let's assume that it is your usual pattern to trade cars every five years You therefore subtract the $3,000 from the annual total in column ⑦ (Transportation), divide the $3,000 by 5 (since it represents a usual 5-year expenditure), and add back the $600 into the Transportation total

More specifically, let's suppose the total annual expenditure in the Transportation column was $4,560, and this included the $3,000 paid out in the car trade The process to work out a normal annual total in column ⑦ would be:

37

God's Managers, a budget guide and daily financial record book for Christians, by Ray and Lillian Bair

ABOUT THE AUTHORS

Craig Hill

Craig Hill, his wife Jan and their two sons, live near Denver, Colorado, U.S.A. where Craig and Jan give senior leadership to Family Foundations International (FFI). This is a ministry through which life-changing seminars are conducted throughout many countries of the world. Craig has also written several books, including the popular *The Ancient Paths*.

Craig holds a Bachelor of Arts (BA) degree from Carleton College in Russian Area Studies and Geology and a Master of Business Administration (MBA) degree from the University of Chicago.

Upon completion of his formal education, Craig worked as a corporate manager in the oil and gas exploration industry for several years. Being an experienced pilot, he later founded and managed a Learjet charter service. During these years, Craig (being fluent in the Russian language) frequently took time off from his business endeavors to minister the Gospel to the peoples of the former Soviet Union and Eastern Europe.

Having a specific interest in ministering to marriages and families, Craig pursued an internship and later a volunteer staff position at the New Life Counseling Center in Denver. He subsequently taught counseling and missions on the faculty of the Marilyn Hickey Bible College. In 1987, the Lord raised up Craig as Senior Pastor of a local church where he and Jan served for seven and a half years, until he was called by God to devote his full-time energy to the ministry of Family Foundations International.

Though his past experience in missions, counseling and pastoral ministry, God has given Craig unique insight into marriage, family, financial and interpersonal relationships. This has resulted in his ability to identify for many people, root causes of relational conflict, compulsive habits, low self esteem, workaholism, lack of financial provision and other undesirable life patterns, which are repeated from one generation to the next. By interweaving personal stories with biblical truths, God has anointed Craig to pierce through the veil of the mind to minister to the depths of the heart, resulting in real life change for many.

Contact information for Craig Hill:

Family Foundations International
Post Office Box 320, Littleton, Colorado 80160, U.S.A.
Phone: (303) 797-1139
Internet: www.familyfi.org

Earl Pitts

Earl Pitts has been involved in full-time ministry with Youth With A Mission (YWAM) for over twenty years. Earl is a director of the corporation, which operates YWAM Ontario, Canada, and is part of the leadership team for all of Canada. Earl and his wife, Dorothy, completed a Crossroads Discipleship Training School and Leadership Training School in YWAM Kona, Hawaii in 1980/81. Each summer for 14 years they have led a Crossroads Discipleship Training School in Cambridge, Ontario. Earl has directed a number of the Leadership Training Schools (LTS) at the University of the Nations in Kona, Hawaii and is involved in conducting leadership seminars and teaching at LTS's in various locations yearly throughout the world. Earl is also on part-time staff of a local church.

He has taught the Biblical Basis for Personal Finances Seminar since 1984 on every continent and has recently been conducting a "Seminar for Businesspersons on Kingdom Assignments" in several countries around the world. This seminar deals with the release of finances and resources for the work of the Kingdom of God.

Earl was employed by the IBM Corporation for 19 years. He began as a graduate electrical engineer and moved through various assignments in project planning, organization and management. His last seven years with the company were spent as Manager of Operations at a manufacturing plant.

Earl and Dorothy have two children. Kendra and her husband with their two children live in Ontario. Scott and his wife, after serving with YWAM in Montana and England, are currently serving on church staff in North Carolina.

This book captures the insights and keys for Walking in Financial Freedom, that have been part of the seminars over the years.

Contact information for Earl Pitts: www.wealthrichesmoney.org